# PROFESSOR AT LARGE

# PROFESSOR AT LARGE

## The Cornell Years

## JOHN CLEESE

CORNELL UNIVERSITY PRESS

Ithaca and London

First published 2018 by Cornell University Press

Printed in the United States of America

Library of Congress Cataloging-in-Publication Data

Names: Cleese, John, author. | Ceci, Stephen J., writer of
    introduction.
Title: Professor at large : the Cornell years / John Cleese.
Description: Ithaca : Cornell University Press, 2018.
Identifiers: LCCN 2018012833 (print) | LCCN 2018019175 (ebook)
    | ISBN 9781501716591 (e-book epub/mobi) | ISBN
    9781501716607 (e-book pdf) | ISBN 9781501716577 | ISBN
    9781501716577 (cloth ; alk. paper)
Subjects: LCSH: Cleese, John. | Cornell University—Faculty. |
    Comedians—Great Britain—Interviews. | Motion picture actors and
    actresses—Great Britain—Interviews.
Classification: LCC PN2598.C47 (ebook) | LCC PN2598.C47 A5
    2018 (print) | DDC 792.702/8092 [B] — dc23
LC record available at https://lccn.loc.gov/2018012833

# CONTENTS

# INTRODUCTION

IT HAS BEEN ALMOST TWENTY YEARS since I received a call from an old friend, Gerri Jones. She had worked as the administrator of the Andrew D. White Professor-at-Large (PAL) Program at Cornell University for many years. Gerri shared with me Professor Porus Olpadwala's dream to have John Cleese be nominated as a PAL. They are appointed for six-year terms and asked to visit campus at least twice for two weeks at a time during their appointments. However, because Porus was chair of the Professors-at-Large program, he was unable to nominate Cleese himself. Learning of this, Gerri asked me if I would be willing to spearhead the nomination. Faculty are asked annually to nominate eminent individuals to be PALs. The typical nominees for these prestigious invitations are scholars, including Nobelists and recipients of other esteemed awards such as Pulitzer Prizes and Tony Awards. And this is how I came to nominate John Cleese (or JC, as we now affectionately call him) to be an Andrew D. White Professor-at-Large.

To say that I immediately resonated with Gerri's request is an understatement. I had never met JC, but like many of my colleagues, I was familiar with his oeuvre. Some of my familiarity resulted from having lived and studied in England for three years during the mid-1970s.

During my time there, *Monty Python's Flying Circus* was erupting throughout the UK, shortly followed by *Monty Python and the Holy Grail* and *Life of Brian*. (It would be a couple of years before the show reached a comparable fever pitch in the U.S. and Canada.) So when Gerri called, I was both cognitively and emotionally prepared to be the faculty nominator of John Cleese.

The rules for nominating PALs call for broad endorsement across the Cornell campus. So I began making calls to colleagues in various disciplines, from mathematics to the social sciences and humanities. I asked them to write supporting letters to accompany my nomination of JC. No one declined and, in fact, everyone was thrilled to be part of the plan. Once I drafted the nomination, it was cosigned by a diverse group of scholars. I submitted it to the committee and the rest is history!

A month later the committee notified me that the nomination was successful, and I was asked to call JC to find out if he would accept the invitation. This was exciting, but also intimidating. I did not know him personally, and I feared he might regard a cold-call invitation, at best, as an imposition on his time. I remember thinking the chance that I would actually reach him by phone was low. Gerri gave me a London telephone number that she said was affiliated with Cleese. I assumed it was an office that he seldom frequented, so I planned to leave a message that might get relayed to him. The person who answered turned out to be JC's personal assistant. I explained to him the details of the invitation, how Cornell would pay for all costs associated with each visit, our expectations for the kind of events he might do, and more. The assistant took notes and said he would make sure Cleese got my message. He wasn't kidding. Within a half hour my office phone rang and it was none other than John Cleese, complete with his famously hilarious voice. We talked for fifteen to twenty minutes and I remember being struck by how absolutely down-to-earth and humble he was. There was nothing pretentious or haughty about him. He told me how honored he was to be nominated and how much it meant to him to be recognized by faculty members of an Ivy League university as a visiting professor. I was bowled over because I had assumed I would have to sell him on the idea. After all, it carried no remuneration aside from his travel costs and, in fact, would mean that he had to forgo work on lucrative films and one-man shows while he was visiting each year. Yet he seemed genuinely thrilled and wanted to know when he could start. He was so keen that he actually started coming to Cornell before his appointment began so he could discuss with us our expectations.

Perhaps I can be forgiven for my low hopes of getting JC to accept the PAL appointment. Cleese was, and remains, a huge talent. Within a few years of our phone conversation, he would go on to be voted by two hundred professional comedians as the second-best comedian of all time, besting Groucho Marx, Laurel and Hardy, Peter Sellers, Steve Martin, and Woody Allen. So this man did not need Cornell to seal his fame. Yet he came to Cornell and put on incredible events, including talks, workshops, and an analysis of *A Fish Called Wanda*. And JC also did something that I had not foreseen: he asked not only to visit classes but to teach them, from script writing to psychology, religion, hotel management, and even medicine. Cleese was also fascinated by much of the research my colleagues were doing, and he often requested to sit in on their classes. They, of course, welcomed him with open arms. Thus, each visit was one in which JC delivered a public presentation, attended and lectured in classes, and met privately with researchers. On one occasion, he dropped in on my lab, which had around fifteen students, mostly doctoral candidates. One of them was British. JC entered the seminar room a few minutes after we began and sat alone. I never introduced him, but my British graduate student recognized him, and the whispering spread like a contagion. When I asked her to describe to JC her research, this extremely articulate person became tongue-tied. It was very amusing to see the reaction that JC had on most students (and not a few faculty members).

After a few years, we added a new feature to his visits, assembling small groups of scholars for informal chat sessions. These proved popular, not only with JC but with the rest of us too. Speaking for myself and Gerri, we attended every one of these sessions and they quickly became our favorite events. JC easily held his own among the scholars, asking penetrating questions on every topic. He has a true scholar's intellect, which perhaps should not have surprised me given his law training at Cambridge University. But even among scholars, it is rare to find individuals with his catholic taste and ease interacting with other academics outside their areas of specialty. JC delighted in these chat sessions. On occasion he would jot down a comment someone made and announce he was going to use it in his one-man show. And he did. Once or twice an idea came out of these chat sessions that we talked about testing. One such idea was JC's own. The faculty group had been discussing synchronization as a biological concept, and Steven Strogatz, the eminent mathematician, was among them. Steve had recently written his book *Sync,* in which he revealed the math behind synchronies in nature. Cleese was triggered by something Steve said and connected it with an observation he'd made long ago in the comedy business. He said that he felt there was a tipping point as far as audiences are concerned: with groups below forty or fifty people, it was more difficult to engender the sort of viral laughter he could evoke in larger audiences. One thought led to another, and before long we had designed an experiment to test JC's hunch. Maybe someday we will get the opportunity to test it.

The term of an A. D. White Professor-at-Large is six years. It is possible to renew the appointment for up to two additional years and we requested this to be done. The A. D. White committee was in full agreement even though it is unusual to reappoint someone, so JC served for two more years, which took him to 2007. During this time, he continued to mesmerize new generations of students, staff, and faculty, filling venues to the point of standing room only. He also occasionally mentioned Cornell during appearances on national television programs, such as *Good Morning America.* As the campus became increasingly aware of how important his relationship to Cornell was, they asked more of him than we had ever asked of other visiting professors. To name a few examples, he made a surprise appearance at the roast of outgoing president Hunter Rawlings, delivered a "sermon" for a Sunday service in Sage Chapel, and made a presentation to the parents of entering freshmen. It was no surprise that he filled Barton Hall.

The sermon at Sage Chapel is included in this book, along with a screenwriting seminar that features an engaging interview with screenwriter William Goldman. The volume also includes several notable lectures: "Hare Brain, Tortoise Mind," on business, "What is Religion?" on the film *Life of Brian*, and "Creativity, Group Dynamics, and Celebrity" with Professor Beta Mannix. In addition, I am honored to have teamed up with Professor Cleese on a lecture about facial recognition, entitled "The Human Face."

As we neared the end of his reappointment, Gerri and I felt that Cornell needed to come up with a more permanent arrangement for JC, who himself wished to continue this relationship. When we raised the issue with the then-provost Biddy Martin, she was enthusiastic, and after some reflection, suggested the rarely granted title the provost's visiting professorship (she had only bestowed it once before) and announced that JC would be appointed to an initial five-year term. The current provost, Michael Kotlikoff, has renewed it.

In the fall of 2017, during JC's most recent visit, he performed a one-man show to a standing-room-only audience at Bailey Hall, introduced by Provost Kotlikoff. At the end, he was led through a Q & A session by Dean J. Smith, director of Cornell University Press, which serves as the final chapter of this book.

I was honored to be asked by Dean to write this brief history, as I believe that playing a part in bringing JC to Cornell has been one of the most significant events in my thirty-eight years here.

STEPHEN J. CECI, Helen L. Carr Professor of Developmental Psychology, Cornell University, December 10, 2017

# PROFESSOR AT LARGE

# HARE BRAIN, TORTOISE MIND

## JOHN CLEESE

APRIL 4, 1999

MAY I SAY HOW DELIGHTED I AM to have been asked to speak to you this afternoon, because usually when I appear in public, it is a show business occasion and I am therefore expected to be funny and entertaining.

So it's a great relief to me to know that there's no expectation of that here at Cornell. So as I have some forty minutes to pad out, I thought I'd start by recommending a book.

It's called *Hare Brain, Tortoise Mind*. It's a book that addresses a danger that has been developing in our society for several years. This danger is based on three separate wrong beliefs. The first is the belief that being decisive means taking decisions quickly. The second is the belief that fast is always better. The third is the belief that we should think of our minds as computers.

Let's look at these forms of insanity in more detail.

First, the belief that decisiveness means taking decisions quickly, that you ask a decisive person a question and [*snaps fingers*] just like that—you get a decisive answer.

Well, let me tell you the most important lesson I have ever learned in my twenty-six years with Video Arts. I learned it when I was writing a film on decision-making. It is this: when there is a decision to be taken, the first question to ask is, when does this decision need to be made?

And that's when you take the decision. Don't take it until then, as new information, unexpected developments, and—perish the thought—better ideas may occur.

So although making decisions very quickly [*snap, snap, snap*] *looks* impressive, it's not only show-off behavior but actually a bit cowardly. It shows that you'd rather create the impression of decisiveness [*snap, snap*] than wait to substantially improve your chances of coming up with the right decision.

Second wrong belief: faster is better.

Of course, I know that this is sometimes true. If your office catches fire, you don't need to call in the whole department to brainstorm before you call the fire brigade. But in business life such urgency is the exception, not the norm. And yet, more often than not, we unthinkingly take it for granted that *fast* is more desirable.

I'd like you to listen to some classical music. [*Beethoven's Fifth Symphony is played for the audience at three times its normal speed.*]

That was the latest, "fast" version. The question is, is it better? Because thanks to modern technology, you can now listen to everything Beethoven ever wrote in just twenty minutes. And that's while eating lunch and riding an exercise bike. Wonderful what we can pack in these days.

You think I'm joking? Take a look at this irresistible offer from American Airline's current mail-order catalog [*shows "Famous Books" advertisement*]:

> The World's 100 Greatest Books Audio Cassette Collection. If you were to read each of these 100 great books at the highly ambitious rate of four per year, it would take twenty-five years to read the entire collection. But now with each book condensed onto a forty-five-minute sound cassette, you can absorb much of their knowledge, wisdom, and insight in just a few weeks and acquire a depth of knowledge achieved by only a few people who have ever lived.

Now there's efficiency for you!

Let me tell you a story. In the 1920s a professor at Oxford and a professor in Beijing communicated with each other by mail for many years. Eventually, the Chinese professor wrote saying that he was coming to visit Oxford. The Oxford professor thought that he would like to show the Chinese professor something quite outside his normal experience, so he took him to an athletics meeting. After one race there was a lot of cheering and excitement, and the Chinese professor asked what it was about.

"Well," said the Oxford professor, "the man in the red shirt has just run the one hundred yards one-tenth of a second faster than it has ever been run before in this country."

"I see," said the Chinese professor, "and what does he propose to do with the time he has saved?"

There is, of course, a point in doing some activities quickly, but there are some processes in which it is pointless to hurry. Hence the Polish proverb, "Sleep faster, we need the pillows." But in corporate and business life in the West today, hurrying has become a sort of mind-set; we do it automatically. Yet after decades of inventing timesaving devices, we have less time than ever to do the things we want. So doing everything faster is not necessarily the answer. Nor, paradoxically, is it necessarily very efficient. Remember the old IBM maxim: don't confuse activity with achievement.

So, second wrong belief in contemporary business is, faster is always better.

Third wrong belief: we should think like computers.

Let me read you what Neil Postman, a professor of communications theory, says about that in his wonderful book *Technopoly*:

The computer, in fact, makes possible the fulfillment of Descartes's dream of the mathematization of the world. Computers make it easy to convert facts into equations. And whereas this can be useful (as when the process reveals a pattern that would otherwise go unnoticed), it is diversionary and dangerous when applied indiscriminately to human affairs.

And later on Postman says that behind our computer culture lies an erroneous assumption that most serious problems are *technical* and generally arise from inadequate information.

> If a nuclear catastrophe occurs, it shall not be because of inade-quate information. Where people are dying of starvation, it does not occur because of inadequate information. If families break up, children are mistreated, crime terrorizes a city, education is impo-tent, it does not happen because of inadequate information.

And if a firm goes out of business because a competitor has come up with a fresh and original idea, the odds are that had very little to do with inadequate information either. So the computer does not help us in these situations. As Thoreau pointed out, technology is simply an improved means to an unimproved end.

These three beliefs—being decisive equals making decisions quickly, faster is always better, we should behave like computers—come together to form the very dangerous idea that the kind of thinking business managers should be using all the time is fast, purposive, delib-erate, logical, computer-type thinking, and that this mode of thought represents the highest intellectual achievement of man.

Codswallop. Horsefeathers. Hogwash. Fiddlesticks. Balderdash. Flapdoodle. And poppycock. To clarify, I disagree.

Because I know that there is a slower, less focused, less articu-late way of thinking that for some problems works much better. Silly example: sometimes people come to interview me about my comedy and ask, "Where do you get all your ideas from?" I always reply, "I get them every Monday morning on a postcard from a little man in Swindon called Figgis. I once asked him where he gets them from and, apparently, it's from a woman called Mildred Spong, who lives on the Isle of Man. But he tells me that she absolutely refuses to say where she gets hers from."

The point is, we just don't know where we get our ideas from, but it certainly isn't from our laptops. They just pop into our heads.

The greatest poets and scientists freely admit that they have no control over the creative process. They all know that they cannot create to order. They can only put themselves in favorable—usually quiet—circumstances, bear the problem in mind, and . . . wait. Indeed, the whole creative process is so mysterious that academic psychologists who studied creativity in depth in the '60s and '70s eventually just gave up because they couldn't get any further—they literally couldn't explain it.

But although we can't explain it, we do have descriptions of what happens. Albert Einstein, for example, said of his own creative process:

> Words do not seem to play any role in my mechanism of thought; I seem to use more or less clear images of a visual type, combined with some almost muscular feelings. These vaguely play together, combining with each other, without any logical construction in words or signs which could be communicated to others.

And a range of Nobel Prize winners agree: "After months of frustration, seeing the solution in a flash"; "It *must* be like *this* . . . it's intuition"; "It's a feeling . . . I must follow this path"; "Not reasoning, not calculating, not making an effort; simply bearing in mind what you need to know."

Okay, okay, all that creative reverie is all very well for Einstein and Shakespeare and Seamus Heaney and the boffins at CalTech, but the rest of us slaving away in our offices have more pressing and practical problems on our minds. True. But it's also true that one of the most pressing and practical problems—often the most pressing and practical problem—we face is, where we can find more innovative ideas and more creative solutions? By putting ourselves in precisely the same relaxed, attentive, open, and inquiring states of mind that I've been talking about.

Because the whole point of what I'm saying today is that it's not just scientists and poets who rely on intuition and promptings from their unconscious. The same is demonstrably true in the business world. And if you talk to really successful innovators in the world of technology and business, you find them describing their major breakthroughs in exactly the same kind of language as poets and physicists. Bill Gates, Ross Perot, Robert Bernstein (of Random House), Joyce C. Hall (of Hallmark), John Teets (of Greyhound), Sir John Harvey-Jones all pay glowing tributes to the power of *hunch* and *intuition*.

These are words that you will not find in the curriculum of business schools, and which in most corporate cultures are treated like the plague, even though we happily rely on them all the time in our everyday lives. For example, we all know the tip-of-the-tongue phenomenon: we can't quite remember a name and the more relentlessly we pursue it, the more resolutely it evades us. Yet if we stop thinking about it, five minutes later it pops effortlessly into our minds. That is not the result of fast, purposive, logical thinking.

And we also know the kind of problem that we need to sleep on. It doesn't have a logical solution like a math problem. It needs us to plumb our feelings, our assessments of situations and people, our intuition—all of which takes time. And the next morning we know how to proceed. A course of action feels right to us although it may take us some time to explain it in words. Please note, in this kind of thinking, the solution precedes verbalization: like all seeds, it needs a period of peace and quiet in which to germinate.

So we all know at a gut level that this slower way of thinking works for us. Yet we don't quite trust it. We somehow believe that the faster mode of thinking is more reliable, more realistic, more respectable, more scientific—despite what scientists tell us! Sadly, most of us believe today that a computer is of more use to us than a wise man.

This is why I was overjoyed to find this book, *Hare Brain, Tortoise Mind*, written by Guy Claxton, an academic psychologist who is familiar with all the psychological research about thinking, and who is therefore able to prove, with hard scientific evidence, that slow thinking is just as valid as fast thinking—for certain problems.

To clarify, by *hare brain* Claxton is referring to the sort of practical, workaday thinking which involves weighing up known pros and cons, constructing logical arguments, using measurements, and consciously solving problems. An engineer working out why a power switch keeps shorting, a project manager checking the cost of materials, a job applicant wrestling with a multiple-choice examination question—all are employing a way of knowing that relies on the application of reason and logic to known data or deliberate conscious thinking.

*Tortoise mind* is the way Guy describes our slower way of thinking: an endangered species in corporate life these days, where the word *slow* has come to be synonymous with *stupid*. Tortoise thinking is less purposeful and clear-cut, makes fewer assumptions, is more playful, leisurely, or dreamy. In this mode we are ruminating or mulling things over, being contemplative or meditative. We may be pondering a problem, rather than earnestly trying to solve it, just bearing it in mind as we watch the world go by.

And he says this: "These leisurely ways of knowing and experiencing are just as 'intelligent' as the other faster ones. We need the tortoise mind just as much as we need the hare brain." In other words, in many situations it offers an infinitely more resourceful and inventive approach to problem-solving than our quick logical, but conventional conscious minds.

Let's be clear: we need both. Because some of the problems we come up against need hare-brain thinking, and some of the problems need tortoise-mind thinking, and some problems need the two together working as a team. Hare-brain thinking works best when the problem is straightforward, logistical, clearly defined. We know what kind of an answer we need, we know what factors are involved, we have all the information we need, and we can rely on the measurements we've been given.

On the other hand, tortoise mind works best in complex, ill-defined situations when we are not quite sure what sort of an answer we are after, where it's not clear how many factors are involved, where we may not have all the information, and where it's hard or impossible to measure the factors. Like a lot of real-life problems—how to manage a difficult group of people at work, how we can best handle a child who is having problems at school, or whether we need a completely new approach to our marketing.

A simple example: If you want to know the fastest, most efficient way to drive from Chicago to Tulsa, hare brain directs you to the freeway. If, on the other hand, you want to know what kind of people live in the Midwest, how they earn a living, what the landscape is like, how the economy is going, and so on—if you want to understand and get a feel for the Midwest—tortoise mind will meander south, follow its nose, explore interesting byroads without worrying where they may lead. You may arrive a lot later, but you'll be a lot wiser.

Because that's how tortoise-mind thinking works—it's curious, open-minded, follows its nose. Unlike hare brain, it has no problem with vagueness or confusion. It looks, without deciding in advance what it's looking for. Because, in Claxton's words, "The fundamental design specification of the unconscious brain enables us to find, record, and use information that is of a degree of subtlety greater than we can talk or think about."

The bottom line is this: hare-brain thinking works well when we need to make smallish modifications in an otherwise satisfactory way of doing something.

Tortoise mind is needed when we are after a really new and creative idea. And Guy Claxton argues that, in this technological age, we've all started to neglect tortoise mind. If you want to get an MBA, you'll find that the entrance exams and the GMAT test to the college will only test your hare-brain thinking capabilities. In business the tortoise is disqualified before the race even starts.

So why is tortoise mind neglected? One reason is that hare brain is articulate. It can explain its thoughts and solutions because it's consciously aware of its own activity. As the math teacher says, you can show your figuring as you go along. We cut the advertising budget, the sales figures went down; therefore, the sales figures went down because we cut the advertising budget. You have a hunch there may be another reason, but you can't quite express it . . . so you forget it.

It's the opposite with tortoise mind. If you're in tortoise mode you can't possibly describe how you are thinking because you've no idea what's going on below the surface of the mind where your intuition resides.

This must be why hare brain has established an advantage over tortoise mind: because hare brain can always sound good and logical. Imagine a situation where two people are contemplating a marketing problem. One is very experienced. This person likes to sense how the marketing campaign might work, feel what's going on, based on years of experience of the firm's customers and previous campaigns. So it may be a long time before his tortoise mind comes up with a hunch that the marketing campaign will work—or won't work. And it will be even longer before the person can articulate the feelings and reasons underlying the hunch.

On the other side of the table is an articulate young person thinking about the same marketing campaign in hare-brain mode. This person may have joined the company last week, may know nothing of the company's customers or previous campaigns, yet this person, having read three books on marketing and having verbal facility, may sound much more persuasive because they express their ideas so well. This kind of executive can fall into a category of manager known as the "articulate incompetent." They're very good at manipulating words and phrases and ideas impressively—it's just that they don't really, really understand what they are describing. But the danger is that they will sound better than someone who does, and we will therefore believe them. So we must not mistrust tortoise mind just because it's not articulate. We must wait for it to express itself before we let hare brain analyze and criticize it.

Now, let's talk about golf. Are there many golfers here? Well, I can give you a useful hint about your putting.

A group of people who were starting to play golf—real beginners—was studied by a psychologist. He was interested in their putting. He divided them into two teams. One team was taught. They were given a set of very specific and sensible instructions on how to putt. The other team was simply asked to practice. No lessons, no instructions; they were told to figure it out for themselves.

After they'd been practicing for some time, the psychologist arranged a putting competition between the two teams. And he deliberately subjected them to stress. First of all, he produced an imposing "golfing expert" to observe, and then he set significant financial rewards and penalties.

Who won? The team that had learned intuitively. They held up much better under pressure than the ones who had received instruction. The psychologist's explanation is that the instructed group was flipping back into hare-brain mode and trying to remember and follow instructions. They were thinking too much. The team that had learnt intuitively couldn't do this—they just played the shot.

And the great basketball player Larry Bird told a friend of mine that the advice the top players often give each other at critical moments is, "Don't think too much—just play!"

Now, what I want to do next is just that—play a little game to demonstrate your tortoise mind's invisible intelligence at work. I say *play* because if you treat what I'm about to show you as some kind of a test, you're going to feel under pressure and start using your hare brains. So you don't have to put your hands up or anything. Just notice how you personally react.

I'm going to show you two groups of words, three words in each group, like this [*a pair of word trios is presented on a screen*]:

A. pal, knife, play
B. still, pages, music

The words in either A or B are related by another common word. The other trio, B or A, is random. So just look at the trios and have a hunch, no more than a feeling, about whether the related ones are A or B.

Okay, let's do this again [*a second pair is presented*]:

A. stick, light, birthday
B. party, round, mark

Here are the two trios. Which trio has related words—A or B?
   Next, try the same again [*a third pair is presented*]:

A. house, lion, butter
B. magic, plush, floor

   Now one last time [*a fourth pair is presented*]:

A. water, tobacco, line
B. sixteen, spin, tender

Which are related? Don't figure out by what. Just have a hunch.
   Now let's go back [*the first pair is presented again*]:

A. pal, knife, play
B. still, pages, music

The answer is A. Did you guess A? And what relates the words is
the word *pen*. But the point is, was your hunch right before you
knew that?
   Next pair [*the second pair is presented again*]:

A. stick, light, birthday
B. party, round, mark

Which trio is related—A or B? Trust your intuition. And the answer
is A. Were you right? And the word that connects A is *candle*.
   Next [*the third pair is presented again*]:

A. house, lion, butter
B. magic, plush, floor

Which trio is related A or B? Answer . . . B. Was your hunch right?
I suspect it was. B are all connected by the word *carpet*.
   And in the last set [*the fourth pair is presented again*]:

A. water, tobacco, line
B. sixteen, spin, tender

The answer was A, and the connecting word is *pipe*.

Okay, now the interesting thing is that almost everyone guesses A, A, B, A without knowing what the connecting word is, and almost everyone's right. This is good news because it means that you know more than you think you do . . . if you'll trust your tortoise mind. So, as other ages and cultures have always known—and incidentally recent neurological studies are now able to prove this scientifically—the unconscious tortoise mind is hugely knowledgeable and intelligent.

But if you're not used to trusting it, it's not so much a question of learning to have hunches, because you have them already; it's much more a question of learning to tune into them better, to take more interest in them.

So what has this got to do with the world of business? Well, most of the real thinking we do at work is either figuring out as clearly as we can what a problem is or coming up with a solution to it.

While we're in the process of figuring out what a problem is, we need to understand it as deeply as we can. That means that if our tortoise mind senses a connection, some factor we've so far missed, it's essential that we don't panic and dismiss it out of hand because we can't immediately explain it. So, provided we have time, we need to let our tortoise mind feel the situation out, take the back roads, sense all the accumulated experience that can be hard to verbalize, and then, when we've explored these hunches, then, and only then, try to put them into words.

Let me express in a different way why tortoise mind is vital to this process. It's because hare brain is a real know-it-all. "Yeah, fine, know this, we can assume that, we all know the other, therefore it's obvious that X, any fool can see that, it's staring you in the face, just look at how confident and miraculously right I am."

Tortoise is not a know-it-all. It's never sure. It's not worried by confusion or apparent contradictions; it's literally open-minded, open to all manner of suggestions. And if something doesn't feel right, if some detail appears out of place, it doesn't brush it aside. It's like a detective—it's curious.

Curious. Because it's curious, playful, and free of preconceptions, the tortoise mind takes you to places that the hypercritical, ultra-rational hare brain would never dream of going. That's why we also need our tortoise mind when we're trying to figure out a problem.

You remember that I mentioned the research done on creativity in the '60s and '70s. The most interesting, for me, was done by a Professor MacKinnon at Berkeley. He studied creativity in various professions, especially architects. He asked lots of architects who were the most creative people in their profession. Then he studied the difference between what the very creative architects did and what the others did. And he found that it wasn't IQ, or any other kind of intelligence; it wasn't how hard they worked. The only difference was that the most creative architects knew how to play with a problem. So when they needed a creative solution, they could switch their minds into a playful mode, where they would just fool around with the problem, chew it over, explore it out of pure curiosity, for its own sake, because they got really interested.

So when we need to innovate, to create, we need to access our tortoise mind. And that involves nothing more complicated than giving ourselves permission to stop trying so hard. To forget for the moment what kind of answer we think we want and just let our brains go soft and chew over a problem in a slightly contemplative, open-minded way, to let the mind wander freely, explore associations and hunches, try things out—without worrying where it's all going.

The problem is that because of our obsession with speed, presentation, and computer-friendly solutions, people find it hard to get into this frame of mind at work. Yet at home we switch ourselves into tortoise mode all the time—when we're relaxing with friends, daydreaming as we listen to music, or making up stories for our children. We don't go running to the database or worrying about deadlines when we're choosing what to have for lunch or deciding who looks the most interesting person at the party. So the trick is to find ways of replicating in the workplace a state of mind we normally leave at home.

How? Before I came here I ran some of these ideas by some of my colleagues at Video Arts in Chicago, and they said, "Great, terrific, all that's missing is a to-do list of practical things people can do to help themselves: take off the pressure, relax, and start listening to their hunches and intuitions."

So here they are: if you want to be more creative and open-minded in your work, 1) stop trying to draw up to-do lists, 2) stop trying to draw up to-do lists, and finally, and most important of all, stop trying to draw up to-do lists. Because the whole point of tortoise-mind thinking is not a trick or a fashionable new management technique; it's something that goes on in all our heads, all the time, whether we want it to or not, but which we have decided to consign to the ghetto of our leisure time. To start using it again, all you have to do is remind yourself it's there and allow yourself the sort of calm and unpressured space in which you can listen to what it's offering you creatively.

The poet Ted Hughes once compared this process to fishing. New ideas are tentative, shy creatures. To coax them out you need patience, time to get a sense of what's happening. Drop a word or an image or a problem into your tortoise mind, let it float there, and see what associations begin to surface.

And that's where ideas come from. Goodbye. [*Cleese behaves as though he's finished the speech. Then he checks, changes his mind.*]

Your tortoise mind's intuition has a hunch it's not that simple? Your tortoise mind's intuition is absolutely right.

Here's the problem. Hare brain bullies tortoise mind. So when they compete, it's hare brain who wins.

Why? Because hare brain has a secret weapon: pressure.

Pressure—whether it's shortage of time, constant interruptions, fear of not producing a result, or worry about the opinion of our superiors or colleagues—it's pressure that stops us accessing our tortoise minds. Any kind of pressure forces the brain to focus more narrowly on finding a quick, articulate, and preferably clever-sounding solution. And the greater the pressure, the tighter the focus, the more narrow the tunnel vision, the more conventional the thoughts.

So if we are to use our tortoise mind, we must, for the time being, avoid pressure. And as there is pressure all around us at work, this means creating a space in which our tortoise mind can feel safe. And the only way to create this enclosure for our tortoise is to set boundaries—physical boundaries and time boundaries.

By physical boundaries, I mean that you need some space which is reasonably quiet, where you can literally or metaphorically close your door to insulate yourself from interruptions and distractions.

By time boundaries, I mean that this space will only work if you set a definite time when the tortoise-mind enclosure begins and a definite time when it ends. And this period of time needs to be as long as you can make it because you can't switch straight from hare brain into tortoise mind. For the first few minutes your mind will race about, thinking about all the phone calls that you should be making and all the shelves that you should be putting up at home. Such anxious mental activity starts to subside after a time, and then the tortoise can come out to play.

So create for yourself an enclosure for your tortoise that is as long as you can afford, by setting boundaries of space and time. And then, to switch metaphors—start fishing.

BUT! WHAT IF THERE AREN'T ANY FISH???

What do you do if you seem to be getting nowhere, if the fish aren't biting? Well, you start thinking, I'm uncomfortable. I'm anxious. I can't do this. I should never have started to try. I've never been creative. I'm a complete failure. I'm going to be fired. And that means my spouse will leave me. In other words, you start enjoying a good old-fashioned panic. Instead of waiting for the fish to come to the surface, you panic and start thrashing the surrounding water with your rods to try to knock them out.

As we all know from bitter experience, the more frantically you worry about not finding a fresh idea, the less likely you are to find one. So when you get anxious—not if, when—just note it and go on anyway. The creativity research I mentioned earlier shows that more creative people are better at tolerating the anxiety and discomfort of not resolving an issue straight away. So just stick at it and try to get interested in the problem for its own sake.

After all, if time does run out and you still haven't come up with anything very innovative, you can always switch back into hare brain again and see what tried-and-tested old solutions you can lash up into some kind of a decision. But at least you've tried, and you'll be surprised at how seldom *nothing* comes up. So create a tortoise enclosure; live with the anxiety . . . Oh! And there is one other kind of pressure.

*Did I do something wrong?* You see, that's the other kind of pressure you need to protect yourself from: the critical judgments of your colleagues. We're afraid that if we switch into tortoise mode we'll look vague, waffly, inarticulate, silly, insane, or that we might even say something wrong.

So you also need to make sure that your tortoise enclosure is one in which your ego, and everyone else's, feels safe, in which it's absolutely clear that everyone in the room is treating what everyone else says, or doesn't say, with friendly, uncritical curiosity. So it's a time when all the normal rules of rational thought, critical analysis, and clever presentation are suspended for the time being, and when no one has to worry about looking or sounding good.

It's really as simple as that: when people feel free from pressure, free to say the first thing that comes into their heads, free to play games, make jokes—when they drop their defenses so they're quite literally unselfconscious—they start being creative.

So the message is fundamentally the same: get the hare brain to lay off by creating time boundaries and ego boundaries. The more you can do that, the more fresh and unusual ideas you'll come up with.

So I hope you now have a sense of how to get your tortoise mind operating. But there is one last shock. Tortoise mind will always produce new ideas. I did not say it will produce new good ideas. It will produce ideas, some of which are brilliant, and some interesting and improvable, and some a complete waste of time, so terrible that they would win Oscars at the Disastrous Ideas Awards.

But don't be alarmed. All I am saying is this: after you have used your tortoise mind, you must use your hare brain to evaluate what tortoise mind has come up with.

Yes, you now need the logical, analytical, critical, hare brain so that you can bring it to bear on the selection of ideas produced from tortoise mind, so that you can sort the wheat from the chaff, the helpful from the unhelpful, and the breakthrough from the potential disaster.

In a sense, although I didn't say so right at the beginning, perhaps we are right when we don't quite trust tortoise mind as much as we trust hare brain, because at the end of the day it's the hare that needs to be brought in to decide which of the tortoise's ideas work.

That's why they are a team. If we only use hare brain, we may look very efficient, we may think and act logically and quickly, but the danger is we may miss those parts of our experience that are hard to articulate or to quantify—and we will never, repeat never, come up with any truly original ideas or any radically different way of doing things.

Whereas if we favor tortoise mind too much, we may waste time meditating on straightforward logical problems, and we may come up with brilliant new concepts that are accidents waiting to happen, ideas which need analysis and perhaps euthanasia by our hare brain.

So to sum up, we have two modes of thinking available. One is suitable for solving problems where we know what kind of answer we want, where the relevant factors are clear, where we have the information we need, where the information really is quantifiable, and where we are confident that we really do not need to look for a radically new approach. For these kinds of problems we use hare brain.

But there is another group of problems where we may not know what kind of an answer we're looking for, where we may not be sure what factors we need to take into account, where we may not have all the information we need, or where the information isn't easily quantifiable—like when it is about people and how they may respond or when we sense that we need a really new way of thinking about things. For these kinds of problems we use tortoise mind.

However, we must remember that whatever tortoise mind comes up with needs time to be articulated. And when it has been articulated, it needs hare brain to check it over.

So before I finish I'd just like to . . . [*looks off*]. Excuse me just a moment. [*Cleese exits. Sounds of struggle and gunshot are heard off-stage. "Colin" enters in Cleese's place.*]

COLIN: Stop this nonsense! Now! This instant! My brother is a deranged and dangerous subversive. You are to forget every word he's told you. If you've taken notes, eat them. Now! And then ask yourself this question: who needs new and innovative ideas? Eh? Answer me that. I know *I* don't. Come up with one and the whole pack of cards comes tumbling down. So stamp out creative thinking now, before it's too late! And here's how. Got your paper and pencils ready?

1. Always behave as if there's a war on.
2. Strangle curiosity at birth. It may spread.
3. Open all meetings by reciting the magic mantra: "The problem hasn't been born that can't be cracked with more data and newer technology."
4. Defend your preconceptions with your life.
5. If you spot a colleague engaging in unfamiliar activity such as wondering out loud or gazing thoughtfully into space, poke them with a sharp stick and accuse them of wasting time.

And finally . . .

6. Make the questioning of timetables and deadlines a capital offense. If you live in a state which does not allow capital punishment, relocate to Texas.

Class dismissed!

# SCREENWRITING SEMINAR

## JOHN CLEESE AND BILL GOLDMAN

OCTOBER 14, 2000

JOHN CLEESE: I first met the legendary screenwriter William Goldman in the late '70s, and we've been friends ever since. He has a really expert view on a number of subjects that fascinate me: why certain movies *work*; the vital importance of a film's story; how screenwriting relates to his other written work, in the theater, as a novelist, and as an occasional journalist; and, most famously, how Hollywood and its star system really works.

It was a no-brainer to ask him to come to speak to Cornell students, especially given his reputation for being extraordinarily generous in giving help and guidance to young writers.

Now, the nice thing about Bill is that he doesn't like anything he's ever written except for *Butch Cassidy* and *Princess Bride*. You just hate going back to your stuff, don't you?

BILL GOLDMAN: Yes.

CLEESE: You just don't like it. Why not?

GOLDMAN: Well, because I wrote it. It's not what you meant, you see. It's one of those things; when you write it's never what's in your head.

I have certain strengths. I have an ear for dialogue and a sense of story, but I tend, because I get bored easily, to over-surprise, and the novels are wildly over-surprised. You know, I'm just terrified people will stop reading me and, when you're aware of your strengths and weaknesses, sometimes it's difficult.

CLEESE: Bill is also famous in Hollywood for having written two books about Hollywood. I have to tell you, if you want to know really how Hollywood works, you need to read these two. The first one is *Adventures in the Screen Trade.* The other one, very recently out, is called *Which Lie Did I Tell?* Tell us where you got that title.

GOLDMAN: I was in Las Vegas with a scumbag producer. We were in his suite and he was on the phone lying about various projects that he had, and he obviously wanted me to listen to him because he didn't move to the other room of the suite. So I perversely picked up *Sports Illustrated* and did not listen to him. I'm reading the magazine, he's just going on and on prevaricating, and finally I hear, "Bill, Bill!" I look. His hand is over the phone and he's saying in a panic, "Which lie did I tell?" He was not embarrassed; he just wanted to be authentic as to which lie he told. Something you must know about Hollywood is that people do lie. Most of what you read about Hollywood is . . . Can I swear?

CLEESE: Yes.

GOLDMAN: . . . is horseshit.

CLEESE: You can do a lot worse than that.

GOLDMAN: I wrote a line once that caught on out there—it is still quoted in the screen trade—which is: "Nobody knows anything." The point of it is that in the movie business, it's always, always, always, except in the case of a sequel to George Lucas or Steven Spielberg, a crapshoot. No one knows what will work.

So what you read is all lies. You read on Monday why a movie is a success or a failure, but no one says it on Friday. It's all Monday-morning quarterbacking.

One of the great shocks of this year is a movie I have not seen called *Almost Famous,* which got the best reviews of the year and is a titanic disaster. It cost $60 million, that's to make. I assume you throw 30 more million on top for marketing. It will do 35 million at box offices in America, half of that goes to the studio, so you take 17 million, and it cost 90 million, so you're talking about a gigantic loss and everybody's asking, "Well, why didn't it go?" And they say, "Well, it was skewed toward this kind of audience or that kind of audience, the blacks didn't want to go, or the kids didn't want to go, or the rock people didn't want to go, nobody wanted to go to the movie." The fact is, the only reason it's a disaster is that people didn't want to see it. All the rest of what they say is lies trying to justify their job.

I'll tell you a great story about my dearest friend, now dead, Ed Nizer, a money manager in Chicago (I know nothing about finance. I never bought a share of stock). I once said to Ed, "Why did the market go down today?" And he said, "Because, Billy, it didn't go up." And I said, "I'm serious." And he said, "So am I." He said, "That's all. No one has any idea what the market will do tomorrow. Warren Buffet doesn't know. They say, 'Well, it went down on news of terror in the Middle East; it went up on news of profit sharing.' That's all horseshit." In Hollywood, they have no idea at all what's going to work, and that's why everybody in the movie business is very scared.

CLEESE: Bill's most famous for that single phrase, "Nobody knows." I want him to tell you about the morning he picked up the newspapers and read all the really bad reviews in the New York press for *Butch Cassidy.*

GOLDMAN: It was terrible. It was just awful. I was walking with George Roy Hill the day it opened and we'd just gotten killed by the New York critics. It was playing then in two theaters in New York and we were walking by the first one and we went in. The theater manager was very happy to see us and we said, "Why are you happy?" It was a Saturday, it opened on a Friday, and he said, "Because we're doing great business and the people love it." We said, "What about the other theater?" He said, "I'll call." When he came back, he said, "They love it there too." George and I parted in the drizzle at 57th and Park, and I remember one of us said, "Maybe it isn't a disaster after all."

Why it got such terrible reviews in New York, I don't know. Part of it was, I think, because of the price of the screenplay. I wrote an original screenplay—now everybody does that, not so common then—and it went for a lot of money. It went for $400,000, an amazing amount of money then. And this got a huge amount of notoriety in all the national press, the thought being, "Why would anybody pay that kind of money for a screenplay when we all know the directors have all of the visual concepts and the actors make up all the lines?" There was a genuine hostility toward the movie, I think, engendered from that moment. The reviews in the rest of the country were wonderful and the reviews in the rest of the world were phenomenal, but in New York it was killed.

CLEESE: Bill's touched on something that I found incredibly interesting when I read *Adventures in the Screen Trade* because he points out that the perception of movies is very much created by the publicity tour. And, on the publicity tour, they never, ever, ever ask the writer, with the result that the director creates the impression that he sort of made up about half the screenplay and the actors somehow manage to create the impression they made up the other half.

GOLDMAN: Here's what an actor would say: If you've written, "There's Evian," the actor would say, "I want Pellegrino." He thinks that means he wrote it. It's true. It drives you crazy. It absolutely drives you mad because, if it's a hit, everybody wants to be connected. The entertainment business is really about one thing—the next job—because we all want to stay close to the fire.

I begin *Which Lie Did I Tell?* with my five years as a leper. From 1980 to 1985 the phone didn't ring. And I say that I could not have survived that in Los Angeles. It would have been too hard. In New York, no one knows who anybody is, no one cares who anybody is, it was fine, but the panic of being around a flop is so palpable in Southern California that everybody wants to stay away from those people. We all want to be close to the fire. And no one knows what's going to work, so we have this terror in the movie business because if you have a big enough disaster, your career is over.

Sylvester Stallone, not a great actor, a very good writer, wrote a wonderful script for the first *Rocky*. He was the biggest star in the world for years and years and now he's unemployable. His newest movie, *Get Carter*, is a stiff and no one will hire him.

When people are "hot" and major stars, it's inconceivable for us—because they are divine and perfect—to think their careers will end. But they all will. No one stays a star except Clint Eastwood. And that's kind of true. Burt Reynolds, for five years, was the biggest star in the world and now, he's not that old, but it's over. That fear of having it be over permeates everything in the entertainment business.

If I seem to be negative, it's because when I was starting out, no one told me what it was like and I believed what I read in the papers, which was not true, and I was damaged early on by certain lies and things that were told me. If I have to disabuse you of the notion that it's all wonderful, that's okay, because it isn't.

It's a very competitive business, and if you can make a movie that works for people, it's magical. It fills me with great joy that *Princess Bride* worked for a lot of people. Mandy Patinkin is a great singer. He does a college tour and does songs and stuff. He told me once that at the end, after he's done all his encores, they're all waiting for him to say: "Hello, hello, hello. My name is Inigo Montoya. You killed my father. Prepare to die." Then he does it and everybody goes nuts. Anyway, it's wonderful for me that you like that.

CLEESE: Now I want to ask this: You've written novels. How many?

GOLDMAN: I don't know. Fifteen, sixteen, something like that.

CLEESE: And some journalism, a terrific book called *Hype and Glory*. Just talk about that.

GOLDMAN: I was a judge at the Cannes Film Festival and the Miss America contest in the same year. I had no idea I would write a book about it, but the contests are about changing lives. If you win at Cannes, your life is never the same. Miss America, the same. So I wrote a book about changing your life, et cetera, et cetera. They're very similar; the events are very similar.

CLEESE: You also wrote one play.

GOLDMAN: If you remember nothing else, avoid the Broadway theater. It is so *hard*, you don't know how hard it is. It is hard enough writing a play, then it's miserable getting somebody to give you the money to put it on. The thing about the movies, which is neat, is they take so long to make, that by the time the movie opens at your friendly Cornell movie theater, you've had six months or more since you did it and so the scars have healed. In the theater, you are rewriting up till the day you open and so when the critics skewer you, there's nowhere to hide. It's just too painful. Anyway, remember I told you that.

Also, don't ever write a long novel. I wrote a long novel once because I'd never tried it. I tend to try to do different things, and it's very hard to write a long novel. It's much harder to write a one-thousand-page novel than just to write a four-hundred-page novel, just in terms of your life.

CLEESE: You've done journalism, you've done novels, you've done a play, you've done lots of movies, you've also written books about sport because you are a sports nut.

GOLDMAN: Yes.

CLEESE: You said to me you think screenplay writing is the hardest, and that everyone you know who's done a spread of writing, as you have, agrees screenplays are the toughest. Why is that?

GOLDMAN: I'm not saying it's the best—we're not talking art here—it's the pacing. Because if this is a novel and I'm as bright as John Updike, I can go five, ten, fifteen pages doing one auditorium scene. If it's a movie, the only way the scene doesn't empty the theater because it's so boring, is if you open it when the auditorium is empty and you have somebody in the darkness put a bomb under a seat. Then we can talk for a long time because they're all going to die. Right? But except for that, a scene like this, talking heads, is boring. You'd leave. You just have to run with a movie.

Storytelling is different. I'm at the age now where I think every-thing is story—I think story is what makes movies work. And the storytelling in a movie, because of the camera being so fast, there's no time, is tricky. There have been very few novelists who've been able to make the jump, very few. Most of them hated it.

CLEESE: Who have made the jump?

GOLDMAN: Joan Didion and John Dunne write screenplays. Richard Price writes screenplays. Help me. Who else?

STUDENT: Sam Shepard.

GOLDMAN: A) He's not a novelist; he's a playwright. B) He hasn't written that many movies. He doctored one; he's written a couple. Yeah, there are a few. For the most part, playwrights are different. You would think a lot of playwrights would be able to do it, more than can, because they are dealing with compression and stuff: the same length of time, a lot of dialogue, et cetera. But novelists, for the most part, don't like it because the other thing is, when you write your novel, if your editor doesn't like this chapter, tough. You have the power to publish what you want. It's your baby. In a movie, it's everybody's. So essentially, no matter *who* you are, you have no control.

CLEESE: I think Bill said something to me like, "Movies are so unfor-giving because any moment when the story is not developing, you're dead."

GOLDMAN: It's awful. One of the things I tell young writers—and I assume there are a couple here—if you're interested in movies—you have to live in the city to do this—go see a movie all day long. Go on the Friday of a new movie, hit the noon show, you'll see the movie. Take a break. At the 4:00 show, you'll see the movie again and you'll like it less because you know what's coming and you begin to be aware of what's going on around you. Hit the 8:00 show. You'll hate the movie. You're so sick of it and what you'll pay attention to is what's going on around you, and what you will find is audiences in that theater and around the world behave iden-tically. They laugh at the same time, they cry, they shriek in fear at the same time, and they go pee at the same time. And the reason they do that is because they're bored, and the reason they're bored is because we, the writers, have misconceived the storytelling. And when you watch a movie and you listen to the audience, which I tend to do, you sense when you've gone off. And it's a very scary thing when you've lost them because, once you've lost them, it's murder getting them back. It's so hard because they're already thinking about their lives outside.

Sometimes movies can be about subjects. I wrote a great disaster, which none of you have ever seen, nor should you, called *Year of the Comet*, which was a romantic-adventure-comedy-thriller about the chase after a legendary bottle of red wine. The opening scene of the movie took place at a wine tasting in London; we knew it wasn't going to be a *big* hit, but we knew we had done something pretty decent. Now, I always sit in the back-left corner at the first screening. No one had seen the movie. Within the first five minutes, fifty people had fled, they hated it so much, and you sit out there and you think, "My God, these people got in for free and their horrible real lives were preferable to sitting and watching the torment that I had given them." No matter what had happened in that movie, it would have been a stiff because people hate red wine and think it's phony, et cetera, et cetera.

But the storytelling is everything, and it's very hard to do it. I wish I could tell you how. There's a great line of Billie Jean King's: "If it was easy, everyone would do it." It's tricky. I've had two great pieces of story that I found. One was about Butch Cassidy, which is a great story, I think. And the other was about the man-eating lions of Tsavo, which was made into a movie that didn't work called *The Ghost and the Darkness*. And one of the reasons that movie didn't work, I think, was *Lion King*. Lions have had a very strange history. They've been gods and they've been vermin. There was a time that you would kill lions in Africa as easily as we would step on a cockroach. Lions are cute now because of *Lion King* and all the rest of it, and nobody, I think, wanted to see the lions get hurt. But who knows? I don't know.

CLEESE: Who is it who said, "Kill your darlings"?

GOLDMAN: William Faulkner. It's a wonderful expression. When you write, he said, you must kill all your darlings because sometimes we get attached to stuff—we have to work hard to make a paragraph or a scene work and we think, I can't lose that.

I wrote a movie once called *A Bridge Too Far*, a very, very long war movie about a battle. The Brits love their disasters. The most famous British disaster is Dunkirk. The second-most-famous British disaster is the Battle of Arnhem and I was given the chance to write the movie. I had never written a war movie. I thought it was a marvelous piece of material. I took it and one of the reasons I took it was, in the Battle of Arnhem the British had awarded five Victoria Crosses, which they are equivalent to the Congressional Medal of Honor. And I knew going in that, no matter how much I screwed up the movie, I had five great action sequences and they would carry me and they would give me confidence.

And then I finally realized the story I wanted to tell was about the cavalry coming to the rescue and the cavalry doesn't get there in time. And once I had seen that, as much as I wanted to keep those fabulous action scenes, they would have died had I put them in, because those scenes had nothing to do with the men who were trapped at Arnhem Bridge and when they are going to be saved or slaughtered.

So "kill all your darlings" means once you've figured out what your story is, you must protect it to the death. And I know it sounds simplistic when I talk about story. I mean, obviously you're going to have all the rest of the stuff that you all know about. But I think if the story isn't there, especially in a movie, it's over for you.

CLEESE: I was going to say that one of the things I learned when making the transition from writing sketches through to writing movies is that in a sketch, once you've set a situation up, if you think it's funny you want to get three minutes of material out of it, so you have a tendency to squeeze every laugh out of that particular three-minute situation. Now, when you get to movies, you kind of have to do the scene in a minute, forty seconds. You cannot sit around squeezing every laugh out of a scene because of this relent-less need to move on, which simply comes from the fact that if you don't keep moving, the audience leaves you. And once they've left you—and you can feel this in the theater as an actor—it's usually because somebody makes a mistake on stage, blows a line, and the audience knows that something's going on and you just feel them go. And if you work very hard, you can sometimes get them back after about five minutes. But in movies, once they've gone, I think it's very, very hard ever to get them back. Why is that?

GOLDMAN: Well, people leave their home to go into a big dark room with strangers. It's an odd thing. And there's an experience that's supposed to happen, I think, when we go to a movie or a play or something—we're looking for something wonderful, I think, for *memories*. We want to remember stuff. We want to say, "Wasn't that great in so-and-so? Wasn't that wonderful in *Casablanca* when he said all that stuff?" And when a movie begins to drift, I think we get angry and we think, "What am I here for? I just hate it."

CLEESE: I think movies have got faster and faster. I mean, when com-mercials first started appearing on television, you had to cram an awful lot of information into thirty seconds and then the audience got used to the fast cutting. So this is sort of mid- to early 1950s, and the movies began to follow suit. Then MTV came along.

GOLDMAN: Let me talk about MTV for a second. My theory about MTV is not that it happened but *when* it happened. If MTV had happened in the '30s and '40s, you would have had Fred Astaire and Gene Kelly or whoever the big movie stars were. They had all been trained. They all knew how to move.

When MTV happened, you had Elton John, who can't do any-thing. This is not to say he's not a gifted songwriter, but he's pudgy and funny looking with glasses and he plays the piano. That's all he does. So you can't just have him say blah, blah; you'll just die, so you cut to this, you cut to the girls going like that, you cut to the pebbles, you cut to the funny glasses. Almost all the rock groups which are on MTV now are not wonderful performers. They're recording artists. They work in studios and they hate their tours. They have to tour because that's what sells their records. So what you have, I think, on MTV, are a lot of artists who are not gifted at performing, so they hide that with a blizzard of cuts. Since the MTV audience is young, and the most faithful movie audience is young, that's the way movies have gone.

CLEESE: There's so much cutting.

GOLDMAN: I used to love previews—"previews of coming attractions" was what they were called when I was a kid. And now when you see them, it's always a bloodbath movie. And it's a blizzard of cuts and I hate it. Now, part of it is my age.

Hollywood is in trouble; they're in so much trouble. If you went to a conglomerate and said, "You can keep all of your other businesses. You can keep your music business, you can keep your television business, you can keep your internet business, but you get to leave the movie business," they would not let you out of the room, they would be so happy. They're all losing fortunes on their movies now. There are too many movies, they cost way too much to make, they cost way too much to advertise, and most of them lose a lot of money. But they're caught in this spiral. They have to continue. Disney has to keep making movies. Disney, basically, has been very successful with their cartoons; people like going to Disney cartoons. But, for the most part, the movie business right now is spooky. If you talk to anybody in the business, they're scared. They're more scared now. I've been in it for thirty-five years and you're going to start reading big articles. Have any of you read articles yet about the theater chains that are going bankrupt? It's huge. Almost all the theater chains in this country are going to die. Now, what's going to happen, I don't know, but right now the movie business is in perilous shape.

CLEESE: Now, if anyone is still interested in writing movies . . . let's move on to the technique and structure and, since I never know what an audience wants to know, does anyone have any questions about the process of writing?

STUDENT: In *A Bridge Too Far*, there's a scene at the end when the soldiers have come near a house, and there's a shot where you see boots moving through the forest. A detail like that, is that something that the director chose or do you write those kinds of details?

GOLDMAN: I don't remember writing that, but I have no memory for anything. Sometimes it's the director, sometimes it's the production designer, sometimes it's the writer. That kind of sense of . . . what are you trying to tell here? Sometimes it's a matter of doing things at the last minute: "Oh, let's do this, we haven't got that." So they'll throw it in. But, basically, that's a detail.

Shall I talk about how I write a screenplay?

CLEESE: Yes.

GOLDMAN: Let's talk about a movie I wrote, based on a novel by Stephen King called *Misery*, for which Kathy Bates won the Oscar. What I do when I accept a job, which is what we are talking about, we're talking about six months of my life and, when I say yes to one, I deliver my first draft after six months.

And what I do is, I'm looking for the story of the movie, which is not the same as the story of the book. Cannot be. Never will. You'll find people who will say, "Well, they weren't faithful." You can't be faithful. It's a whole different art. So what I do is I read and reread and reread the text. I read it five or six times over a period of several months, each time with a different color pen. And when I find something that I think would be in the movie, I mark in the margin. What I'm really doing is building up confidence. The big terror for everybody is you think it's over. You're trying to build up your own confidence. "I'm going to do something of quality this time," that's what you're constantly trying to tell yourself. By the time I've read the book a half a dozen times, it looks bizarre. It's filled with colored marks. But by that time, I have a sense of what I think the story is.

In the novel *Misery*, very briefly, Jimmy Caan is a famous romance writer, a male Danielle Steel. He's in a terrible car crash in Colorado. He is rescued by a nurse who, it turns out, is his number one fan and it also turns out she's crazy and eventually will try to kill him, but she brings him back to life. In the novel, you know on the first page that he hates her, that she's crazy, and that she's dangerous. When Rob Reiner and I were discussing the storytelling of the movie, the decision was made to delay the knowledge that Kathy Bates was nutty and dangerous for a half an hour of the movie. If you see the movie, you'll see, for the first half hour, she's adorable. She's just sweet and cute and wonderful because we felt, once she turns, you can't go back. So that's a change. King likes the movie, but it's quite different from the book.

Anyway, I then try and write very briefly twenty-five or thirty words, which I'll put on my wall, which is the spine of the piece, which is the story. In other words, the King movie opens with Jimmy Caan finishing a novel, getting in his car in Colorado, driving, getting caught in a storm, having an accident. So I wrote, "Blizzard." That's the first five or eight minutes of the movie. Then I wrote, "Rescue." That's when Kathy Bates comes. And then I work down and, once I have that thing on the wall—I tape it to the wall, literally—that's the movie. The rest of it then becomes a matter of rote work. The hard part is reading and rereading or researching and trying to figure out what is the story we're trying to tell in this case. Because in King's novel there are marvelous scenes of the romance novels that he wrote, which she loves. And in the first draft, I had some of those and we just felt they didn't work. They're wonderful in the book, but it's such a shift. Movies are so real that, once you go into a different color and a different thing and people start talking differently and you're back in the eighteenth century and you're into a bodice ripper, it's a whole different world. So we cut it.

*Maverick* was a Western that I wrote because I thought it would be easy. Really dumb. What I thought was I'd go look at all the James Garner *Maverick* shows that ran an hour and I'd find one that had a great plot and I'd expand it. But what I realized when I watched the shows was they had no plots. They were all based on James Garner's charm, so I had to make up a story. Well, it's about a gambler. So I made the decision that it had to end with a big card game. And once you have that, then you know essentially where you have to begin.

Those decisions cripple everything or make everything. Those are the most important decisions you make. Movies are not about snappy dialogue. It helps if the people are supposed to be intelligent, but that's not what movies are about. Movies are about making the story work on camera—making it be as surprising and interesting as you can for the audience who has come for the night. Anyway, that's how I do it. Does that make any sense?

CLEESE: Tell us about the ending. You see, I think a lot of people sit down to write screenplays and they literally write, "Scene One," and they start writing from the start. I'm sure that some great art is being created in that way. I mean, if you have Charles Dickens or Dostoyevsky or anyone who does writing installments for magazines, that's how they did it. They didn't have time to figure out the whole thing and that's why I think sometimes—

GOLDMAN: The Coen brothers write that way.

CLEESE: Do they?

GOLDMAN: The Farrelly brothers write that way. The Farrelly brothers don't actually mind getting in trouble 'cause they figure if they can get into a spot where *they* can't figure how to get out of it, *you* won't be able to figure how they're going to get out of it either. Then they have the problem of trying to get out of it! But the Coen brothers will just go ahead and write and I don't know how you do that because, in my case, I have to know where I'm going.

The hardest single thing for me on a movie or on anything is the ending. I've only had one fabulous ending and that was *Butch Cassidy*, and that's because it was real life. I could just use what happened. They were attacked by this huge bunch of people with guns.

But endings are so hard. What you hope is that you will get away with it. One of the reasons *The Sting* is one of the great hits of all time is that the last ten minutes are the best ten minutes. If you can make that work, if you can make the last minutes of a movie a crescendo—I don't mean a bloodbath, I mean a crescendo—you'll have a hit.

CLEESE: Those are the ten minutes when you leave the theater that you remember best. And if they're really exciting, if you get them right, it colors your impression of everything that you've been watching that evening.

GOLDMAN: A great actress of the '30s, '40s, and '50s, Rosalind Russell, once said that what made a movie work was "moments." It was Cliff Robertson who told me that story, and he said to her, "What do you mean?" And she said, "If there are three or four moments in a movie that an audience can take away with them, they'll forgive you anything and like the movie."

We all know, we don't know why, but we all know that talent tends to cluster. Shakespeare was not the only playwright in the 1600s; there were a lot of guys in Greece all those years ago, a lot of wonderful American novelists in the '20s and '30s, a lot of wonderful Russian novelists a hundred years ago. We don't know why that happens.

I believe right now, and I have no idea why, and I don't know that I'm right, that in all the arts, this is a time of low talent. I don't think there's a plethora of great choreographers or Italian tenors or movie directors or screenwriters. I think right now is a time of low talent, and that's one of the reasons I think I find movies right now disappointing, maybe because I'm too old, but I don't think they're as good as they were. This is not a golden age for novelists either, I don't think, or playwrights. It's just not a great time. In two or three years, it may all be different. If a burst—we all ride on bursts of young talent, and it would be fabulous if half of you students were really brilliant because then we could have this marvelous golden age in five years or ten years. But we don't know that's going to happen. It's a tricky time.

CLEESE: Well, I wanted Bill to talk about the ending because the only thing I know anything about writing is comedy and I think that the ending is all-important, and I cannot see how you can start from the beginning and work your way through and come to an ending. I can't. But what I'm also fascinated about, and I got this really wrong, was the beginning of movies because I thought, "Well you've got them in the movie house, you know, it's not television. You have to grab them immediately in television, or after a minute they've changed channel. But, they're not going to leave the movie house and go to another movie house after three minutes if they're bored." So I thought you could get into movies in a fairly leisurely way. Now I think that's wrong, so I want you to talk about the beginning of movies.

GOLDMAN: Well, I think a lot of people think that the most important part of any movie is the first five or ten pages of your script because you have that long, for the most part, to set up the world you're going to deal with. And if you do that incorrectly, if people are confused, if people are bored, if people are angry, you're not going to *get* them. So, you don't have a lot of time. The opening of a movie is so important.

I'll talk for a moment about the opening of *Butch Cassidy*. We had two stars in the movie. We had Robert Redford, who was unknown, and Paul Newman, who was Tom Cruise. You all know this is about two guys who go to South America and die, okay? In a lot of movies where there is a big star and an unknown, the unknown goes riding off to get water while the big star fights all the bad guys 'cause that's what big stars do—they get all the good juicy things. It was crucial that the audience realize that Redford was going to stay with Newman throughout the movie. What Hill did, which was just brilliant, was the first time you see Redford is in a card game. It's not a terrific scene, alas, but it's a card game, and someone is about to accuse him of cheating and they don't know who he is and there's a close-up on Redford as the card game goes on. It's a shot on his face that's ninety seconds long. It may be the longest single close-up I've ever been involved with, maybe anybody's been involved with. What he was doing sublimely, he was saying: He's not going away. Watch this guy. But that was the important part.

We had two important parts of the movie to establish early. One of them was there were two guys, not just the one. If we'd had Marlon Brando in the Redford part, the card game shot wouldn't have been there. You would have known: Paul Newman/Marlon Brando, Paul Newman/Steve McQueen. You don't need to establish that, okay?

But the really crucial thing in the movie was they ran away. Westerns are based on confrontation. They ran away. They went to South America because they knew they'd get killed if they stayed in America. That's spooky because Western heroes don't do that.

When the movie went up for auction, every major studio but one wanted it. They all bid, which is why it went so high. And the one that didn't want it said he would buy the movie if they didn't go to South America but they stood and fought the super-posse. And I said, "But they didn't do that." And he said, "I don't give a shit." He said, "I only know this: John Wayne don't run away." Well, that's true, John Wayne don't run away, and my problem, as the writer in trying to make the story work, was to make you want them to do something that was essentially weird in a Western, which was leave. So I invented the middle third of the movie, which is a chase when the super-posse chases them and makes their life harder and harder and harder and finally they jump off a cliff and decide to leave. All that was conscious on my part. I wanted the audience to say, "Get out of here." In real life, there was a super-posse. In real life, when the Newman character heard about it, he fled because he knew they were going to kill him. I couldn't have that. All that thirty minutes is a plot point building to this: please leave. And it worked in that movie. I mean, theoretically it was an exciting chase, but the fact is, that's all it was there for—to try and push the story line to make it all right for them to run away, which Western heroes never do.

CLEESE: I want to take you back to the beginning again and this phrase of yours, I think you say, "The beginning of the movie is where you set up your world."

GOLDMAN: The opening shot of the movie, the audience immediately knows a great deal. We know I'm in a college somewhere, we know people dress a certain way, we know the time. We know it would be unlikely for everyone to pull out machine guns and begin firing. So, if I have that as my second scene, if all of a sudden eight people pull out machine guns, people would say, "Wait a minute. Is that a college? Is that a joke? What are we doing?"

People get very nervous. One of the things I like to do in a movie theater is to watch people's movements because, when they're watching a movie and they're with it, they're with it. And when they're bored, they begin doing things. Their body posture changes if they don't like what they're being told. Either it's the wrong people are on screen, the wrong information is being given by the wrong people, the wrong information is being given by the right people, people don't care about the information, people don't want to see that scene, it's in the wrong order. All this drives you nuts because you're trying to figure out, for a movie to work, how do I make it so that I can lure you?

CLEESE: So you have to establish quite early—

GOLDMAN: *Very* early. I have to tell you what the parameters are. I have to tell you it's funny, it's okay to laugh; it's sad, it's okay to cry. Whatever it is, I have to set up that world immediately at the head of the story so you'll begin to say, "Oh, I see, no one's going to die," or, "This is where a girl has cancer." And when you begin to mix genres, you get into trouble.

STUDENT: I've been wondering what the difference is between writing a beginning scene for the stage or for a movie.

GOLDMAN: In a play, it's all the playwright. In a play, you're dealing with getting a bunch of people in a realistic situation. The lights go down and you're going to tell them some kind of story that will interest them, and it all depends on the writer's skill. You're not going to have special effects, you're not going to have crazy things, you're going to have basically a bunch of people talking and something's going to be learned.

In a movie you can go anywhere, literally go anywhere. Boom, boom, next shot you're in China. You can't do that in a play. The camera in a movie dictates everything, *everything*.

In the theater, it's the writer's words. One has very little to do with the other. Did Tennessee Williams write movies? Not very happily. Arthur Miller didn't write movies happily. It's a whole different world.

A movie is a group endeavor. We're all at each other's mercy in a movie. If I write a terrific script and the director only took the job, which happens a lot, because he needs the money for his divorce payments, and he really wants to direct apples and I've written oranges, well, it's too late. You're going to have a movie that doesn't work.

One of the great directors of all time was David Lean (*Lawrence of Arabia, The Bridge on the River Kwai*). Lean could do size. It's very hard to do size, as most directors don't want to do it. It's like an army campaign. Most directors like dealing with people in a room. Everybody has different strengths and weaknesses.

CLEESE: The thing is, I suspect, is the big difference in the expectation of audiences in the theater. Take something like *Rosencrantz and Guildenstern Are Dead*, Tom Stoppard's play. Tom made a film of it, directed it himself, and was very happy with it. I don't think anyone even knows it was made into a film.

In the theater, people are prepared to go and listen and to hear ideas and to think. Take Michael Frayn's play *Copenhagen*. I think it's the best play I've seen for ten years. It's fantastic. But I think if you put that on a screen, it would die. It's people talking to each other and it's about ideas, and that's not what movie audiences want. Maybe they used to. Bill, did they ever? Because when I went to see *Rear Window* when that was re-released fifteen years ago, I was astounded at how much there was of just Jimmy Stewart and Grace Kelly sitting around talking to each other. And I suddenly thought, "Oh, this must have been a stage play." But when I saw it in the '50s when I was a kid, it didn't strike me as being talky and slow at all. Can you comment on that?

GOLDMAN: A lot of it also has to do with the audience. The movie audience is fifteen to twenty-five. At fifteen, you want to get out of the house. At twenty-five, you begin getting married and having kids. A movie is a cheap form of entertainment. Young people don't go to the theater. They don't like being forced to go at eight o'clock; they don't like being scrunched in that crummy area, they can't talk, here's no popcorn, there are real people up there. It's very expensive; it's $75, not $7.50.

What movies are has to do with who's going to the movies. There was a time in the '50s and '40s when there was a thing called "ladies' matinees." That's before women worked so you would have movie stars who would do tearjerker movies that had huge audiences with women coming to see those movies in the afternoon. Women don't go to the movies anymore, very rarely.

The reason there are so many black-violence films, young blacks are the most faithful movie audience they have. They go to the movies. They just do. People of forty, for the most part, don't go to the movies. People of sixty never go to the movies. When you talk with people my age, they haven't seen a movie in three years. They'll watch it on television, but they don't go. It's a whole different thing.

In the theater, you're dealing with an older, arguably a more staid, and certainly a much more educated audience. When you go to the movies, it's a bunch of kids sitting around having popcorn wanting excitement, and it's a different kind of excitement than it is in the theater.

CLEESE: I think it's important to decide early on what it is that you want to write and then make sure that you're writing it for the correct kind of medium because if you want to write about ideas, it's unlikely that you're going to have much luck in the movies. It occasionally happens, doesn't it? I'm thinking, Tom Stoppard with *Shakespeare in Love*. Now, let's have some questions from the audience.

STUDENT: How many times have you written a screenplay and then seen the movie and said, "Wow, that director is so much smarter than I." Or you didn't agree with how different it is from what you had written?

GOLDMAN: Well, both happen every time you go to see a movie. It's always different. When I'm home, okay, I'm writing about you guys. I say, "We're at a Cornell auditorium." Right? It looks different in my head. If I were to write this scene now, I would use this auditorium and I would describe it with those beams, et cetera. Let's say the director can't get this auditorium so he shoots one in Los Angeles. It will look all different: it won't be brick, it will be wood. It's always different. When you shoot a movie, you never get what you want. You're always limited: what scenes can we shoot in the auditorium, how much is in our budget to dress kids, can we have a hundred kids or do we have to have fifty, should it be in a classroom? You're dealing with all kinds of problems that are around every movie but shouldn't be essential to the movie.

CLEESE: But they're the problems that everyone wants to be involved in. The last thing that people think about is the script because the script is really difficult so you have to sit quietly and really think. As the philosopher John Searle once said, "People will do almost anything rather than think." So people would much rather run around frantically looking at lots of auditoriums, deciding which one would be best. Everyone wants to do that kind of easy thing. Everyone want to speculate about who would be the right actor. There are certain easy things to do and that's always where the energy goes. The script gets forgotten.

GOLDMAN: When I was twenty, I was desperate to be a writer. What one wanted to write was the Great American Novel. That's what everybody wanted to write in those days, and you wanted to write for Broadway if you had a touch of glamour. Those of you who have leanings toward writing or are writing, I would guess that almost none of you want to write for the theater and that almost none of you want to write novels. I would guess that basically what people want to write now is they want to write movies or TV—TV, because movies have gotten so limited that a lot of people right now are writing for television because there's really good stuff on television where the writer has control. If you work for HBO and you are a writer, you have control of that script. The writer is the producer is the director. That's a whole different world. That didn't used to happen. It's all changed now.

A show of hands of people who want to write the Great American Novel. You do? Okay, a couple of you. Well, I think that's fabulous. I don't know, in twenty-five years, if people will want to write movies at all, but they'll all want to write for the internet. I have no idea.

CLEESE: I don't like acting in movies. It's like being at school again. You have to get up very, very, very early, work long hours, and then go home and learn lines instead of homework. And I think what is great about being a writer is you work hard, but at least you can get decent coffee and sit somewhere comfortable most of the time.

GOLDMAN: There's something else. Spencer Tracy, who in the '30s and '40s was thought of as being the great American actor, has almost slid off the radar screen. Through the '50s, Tracy felt that acting was an unmanly occupation for a man. He felt being a movie star was demeaning and so, for the last fifteen years of his very great career, he only took parts where he could dress at home and drive onto the set and go to work. What he hated was, this is what happens: I'm acting and the director says, "Cut," and, "We'll do it again." Okay? While I'm getting ready to do it again, eight technicians come up and they begin to mop me here and they begin to do this to my hair and they do this to my shirt and the whole thing. And Tracy felt that was unmanly and, in many ways, he's right.

CLEESE: I hate it. And I'll tell you another thing. Can I give a quick demonstration [*picks two students*]? I just want you to imagine that you're the actors. Okay. Just the two of you and I'm the director. This is what happens at the end of the take: "Cut!" [*Turns around, ignores the actors, talks to other people inaudibly, and finally turns back to the actors.*] "Right, we're doing it again." And the actors say, "Was the acting all right?" The director goes, "Huh?"

If you want to be a film writer, look at Iz Diamond, who cowrote most of Billy Wilder's films with him. He came on set because Billy wanted him there, and the great thing was he knew that Billy was not going to change a thing—which is what normally happens when a writer hands a script over to a director—because they'd written the screenplay together. And he kind of piggybacked himself into the best possible position for a writer. An old Hollywood joke is about the Polish starlet who came to Hollywood and she knew so little about the way the place operated that she slept with the writer.

GOLDMAN: I want to go back for one second to Spencer Tracy's idea that being a male movie star is an unmanly thing to do. One of the things that I love reading is about the stars who do their own stunts. Let me tell you this: they never have and they never will. Three people have done their own stunts: most recently, Burt Lancaster, Jackie Chan, and Douglas Fairbanks Sr. did their own stunts. Nobody else does because they're dangerous.

I have a friend who was on a Stallone picture years ago and there was a very hairy scene where he had to take a helicopter on a ladder up to one of the bridges in New York, where there was a stalled trolley car, one of those things, and the villain was in the car. A *New York Times* reporter was there and Stallone came over and said, "I want to do that stunt." Well, he would have died if the director had said, "Fine, you're going to do it." Because he would have gotten killed doing it. The fact is, the stupid *New York Times* reporter—all *New York Times* reporters in the entertainment world are stupid—wrote about how obsessed Stallone was. The fact is, the director would have lost his career. Let's say he let him try it. Let's say he got hurt. Stars aren't prepared to do the kind of physical activity that stunts require, but, because it is unmanly, they pretend they do.

CLEESE: More questions. Yes?

STUDENT: Mr. Goldman, you were talking a little bit about how you wanted to be a writer. I was wondering about the moment when you first thought you were going to have a successful book.

GOLDMAN: I wrote a lot of stories. I got infinite rejections. I took a creative writing course at Oberlin, where I went, thank God. Everybody got As and Bs. I got the only C. I took a summer school course at Northwestern. I got the worst grade in the class. We had a literary magazine at Oberlin. I was the fiction editor. Everything was submitted anonymously. There were three of us: the fiction editor, the poetry editor, the overall editor. I would submit my stories, we'd all read everything, and when we came up to my story, they would always say, "We can't publish this shit." So, I could not get my stories in a magazine where I was the fiction editor.

I am twenty-four, I'd finished graduate school, I'd finished the army, and there was nothing left for me to do. I got one offer to teach at Duluth, I think for $2,900 a year, and I didn't want that. I was asked, as I'm from Chicago, to work as a copywriter in a Chicago ad agency, which is not what I wanted with my life. I wanted to be in New York.

When I was very young, for some reason we got the *New York Times* on Sunday, and I remember going through hundreds of pages of "Arts and Leisure" and looking at them thinking, "I must live there." I went to Columbia because it's in New York, among other reasons. Anyway, when I was twenty-four, no one thought I had any talent. No one said, "Fuck those story editors, they don't know, these are really good stories." Everybody said, "Well, you know, it's nice that you're writing but . . ."

So, I'm twenty-four, and I went back to my hometown of Highland Park and I wrote in three weeks a novel called *The Temple of Gold*. I remember being terrified because I'd never written past page fifteen and suddenly I was on page fifty and page eighty and I didn't know what I was doing. But I somehow, in some despair and panic and desperation, knew this was my shot. I wrote this book and a guy I'd been in the army with had met an editor who had become an agent. I sent it to this agent, and he gave it to an editor who he knew, and the editor did not say, "Yes, I will publish this." He said, "I have no idea if you can write. Double this in length, show it to me again, and I'll read it again." Which I still think is weird.

I doubled it in length and I was living with my brother, now dead, who wrote *Lion in Winter,* and with John Kander of *Chicago, Cabaret,* and *New York, New York.* We're all living in an apartment on the West Side of Manhattan. This is the middle '50s. I'm alone, my brother is up in Boston, John is out giving music lessons, and the phone rings and it's the agent saying that Knopf had accepted my book. Knopf was then, maybe even now, the best publishing house in America. I went into a catatonic state. I froze and I began wandering around the apartment, I don't know for how long. And then, Kander came in and said, "Have you heard?" And I said, "Yes, they took it." And he said, "Oh, that's wonderful. Is everybody excited for you?" And I said, "No one knows. I didn't tell anybody." And he realized that I was in very deep shit and he said, "Would you like me to tell people for you, Billy?" And I said, "How would you do that?" And he said, "Well, we could sit by the phone and you could tell me who you wanted to know and I'll call them and say, 'Billy's book was accepted by Knopf and he's a little strange now but he'll be fine tomorrow.'" So we went through a list of all the people I wanted to know, John would dial and say, "Sarah, Bill's book was accepted by Knopf." And then he would put the phone here and I would say, "Isn't that great." And she would say, "Oh, that's wonderful." And the next day I would call her. I still remember that because it was life-changing. Suddenly, I was a writer, and I guess that's the answer to your question. I still don't think I'm talented. I still think I'm fooling them. I still think, each time, that I've gotten away with it. I think that's not abnormal for a writer.

CLEESE: It's not abnormal for actors either. Bill was talking to me earlier about Kevin Kline. What did Frank Rich say?

GOLDMAN: Frank Rich said that Kevin Kline was the glory of the American theater. That was when he was doing a lot of stage work.

CLEESE: I saw Kevin's *Hamlet.* I saw it twice in three nights, and the second was better than the first and the first was the best *Hamlet*

I've ever seen. He made me cry, he made me laugh, and I thought it was extraordinary because I occasionally, very occasionally, like Shakespeare when it's great, and most of the time, I don't like it. But when I said to Kevin afterward, "Well, you've played *Hamlet* in New York, you got very good reviews, very good box office. What do you feel about it?" He said, "Hmmm. I think . . . I got away with it." And it's very strange to me that a lot of the very best people always have this feeling, "Hmmm. I got away with it." And I think the reason is this: if you are creative, you're always, every single time, you're going into unknown territory and you cannot guarantee that it's going to work. You want a guarantee it's going to work? Then just use a formula. Just do something derivative, same as you did last time. It won't be a disaster and, of course, it won't be very interesting. But if you're really trying to do something new each time, trying to stretch yourself, you never know when it's going to be a disaster, so you always feel, I don't really know what I'm doing. And if it comes off, you just feel you're lucky.

GOLDMAN: One of the things that I tell young writers when I start to work with them is that I don't know what I'm doing. It's very important that they realize that. I mentioned *Year of the Comet*, where fifty people left the first five minutes. If I knew what I was doing, why would I write a movie where fifty people would leave in the first five minutes? It wouldn't be smart. And the fact is, I think, once you think you know what you're doing, it's over.

I remember the most famous, exalted, and written-about American figure in the arts of the '90s was Quentin Tarantino, who did a couple of nice movies, a terrible movie called *Jackie Brown*, and has not now done anything in several years when everybody is desperate for him to do whatever. I read an interview with him when he was doing *Pulp Fiction*, where he said—you know that wonderful scene where Travolta is dancing with Uma Thurman—he said, "I didn't know I was a great director until I did that scene." And I thought, "Jesus, it's your second movie and you already think you're great. Where do you go from there?"

One of the things that happens in Hollywood is that people are overpraised. And all of us, basically, are nerds! I'm serious. I don't think people in the entertainment business dated the cheerleader. I don't think so. I don't think even the actors did. I think we were all strange, you know, nerdy. And I think, suddenly when people tell you you're wonderful, you want to believe that so badly and, in Hollywood, you do and your careers are over.

I remember a time, not many years ago, when the three great young directors were Coppola, Friedkin, and Bogdanovich, and if you look at their careers, and these are greatly gifted people, they've essentially done shit for twenty-five years. And I don't know why, compared to the wonderful work of their early careers. It's not that they lost their talent, it's that somehow in the movie business—and it affects all of us—ego gets into it. But I think ego is a big thing, and directors are given so much control, and they don't know how to deal with it. I think most of us, basically, don't know what we're doing, and I think the minute we think we do, it's over. Whenever I meet anybody—and I've worked with a lot of famous people over the decades—whenever they're just arrogant, I just think, "Well it's finished."

CLEESE: Well, I'm not going to tell you how I became a writer. I'm going to tell you how I decided *not* to be much of a writer. It's because I realized many years ago that it's very hard to be a writer *and* to have a proper life.

I think that if you are going to be a writer, what you've got to accept is that you have to create huge chunks of writing time when you don't do *anything* else because the sad thing is, writing doesn't really happen until it becomes obsessive, until it begins to take you over and nag at you. And I think you have to decide: am I prepared to pay that price? Most of the time, I'm not, and most of the time, Bill has.

GOLDMAN: One of the things you have to realize if you want to write, it is . . . a bizarre life. Being a writer means you are essentially going into a room by yourself day after day to do it. And whoever the people were who made you decide to be a writer, it wasn't Jacqueline Susann, it wasn't Danielle Steel. You don't do it because of those people. You do it because of people who somehow moved you or transported you when you were twelve or eighteen or twenty-two. And you know you're not that good. But you have to go into your own little pit alone, alas.

I talk to myself all the time. I didn't know that I did. I was writing a movie called *The Great Waldo Pepper*, and we had rented a house in Massachusetts. The architect had designed the house that literally had very few walls. I was coming in to have lunch one day with the family, and the kids were giggling and I said, "What are you laughing at?" And they said, "You know, you talk when you write." I said, "I don't do that." And they said, "Yes you do." And I said, "No I don't." And then they started quoting the dialogue I'd been writing.

CLEESE: You have a question?

STUDENT: You talked about if you are trying to adapt a novel, you can't adapt it faithfully enough because certain scenes won't work and you can't make how you divide time in a novel the same way in a movie. How can you indicate on a page how long you want a scene to go on?

GOLDMAN: When you are writing, you sense—I do anyway—you sense, "God, get on with it. Do we need to know that the Buick's in the garage?" And if you do, because someone is going to steal the Buick, then you'd better have that nifty dialogue. You write how Buick rhymes with something else because you saw an ad on television. But if you don't need to know that, get rid of it. Movie writing is about connectives: this scene connects with that scene connects with the next, and there's a kind of inexorable thing that happens as it rides you along toward the climax of the movie. That's hard to get right. Anything that stands in the way, you've got to get rid of. Sometimes your best writing is what stands in the way of it, which is when Mr. Faulkner's "kill all your darlings" comes into play. It's just you have a sense—I don't know, I have a sense—that this is *dull*. I get bored. Sometimes I'm reading my own stuff and I think, "What is this? Get rid of it." Because you want to get on to the next surprise, the next wonderful moment for the people sitting out there in the dark.

I wanted to tell one more story about me talking to myself. I used to work in an apartment building in New York with very thin walls, and there was a European lady shrink who lived in the next apartment and we never spoke. Then one day, we're waiting for the elevator, she whirls on me and she says, "I just want you to know, I know everything that's going on in your apartment." Now, sad to say, nothing was going on in my apartment, but I realized a bit later it was this scene I wrote for *Marathon Man*. It's an evil scene where the villain is tormenting the hero saying, "Is it safe? Is it safe? Is it safe?" And I guess I had been screaming. That's what I mean when I say that I talk when I write. The reason why I talk when I write is it's lonely. You want some company. I mutter a lot. I'm terrified I do it on the street. I try not to. But when I'm alone, I'm muttering all the time because I get lonely, physically lonely.

CLEESE: By reading your lines out loud, you have a double chance of seeing whether they work or not—because trying to assess them just on the page, I can't do that. But if I hear the line, I think, "Eh, it's got too many syllables in it, it's not crisp enough, or it ends on a downbeat." You can hear it.

Let me say something about "kill your darlings." This is not supposed to be patronizing, but when you're young and you haven't written so much, you tend to really love what you've written. And when you kind of get old and tired and disillusioned and you're about to die, like Bill and me, then it's much, much easier to throw stuff away because you know you can easily write something else.

Let's have another question.

STUDENT: You've talked about writing individually, but what about collaborative efforts? Especially with sketch comedy, it seems to me that there would be a benefit to do that with someone else.

CLEESE: Bill, have you written much with anyone else?

GOLDMAN: A little bit. I find it heaven. You're not alone; you have someone else to talk to. I love that. I love the socializing. I love getting into conversations. A lot of comedy is written in tandem, isn't it?

CLEESE: Well, it's so difficult to tell whether something is funny and a partner can be reassuring. On a movie, there's another problem. Here's a brief breakdown on how many times you laugh on a movie:

A movie, if you're lucky, takes two to four years. Let's say if you're in from the beginning—you know, you're developing a script, setting up the production, shooting, editing, then doing publicity. It's an awful lot of time. So the first time, let's say Bill and I are writing the script and we think of something funny and we laugh. Okay? And then when we look at it the next day, we giggle again. Well, the next time we get to laugh at it is when there's a read-through a year later and everybody laughs at the joke. And then, maybe, two months later when you're shooting it, it's kind of funny while you rehearse it the first two or three times. And then, you might laugh at it in rushes, and then, when the whole movie is edited together, you might laugh at it again when everything is absolutely right and it's all cut beautifully and the sound is mixed and it's perfect. So, you might laugh at that joke on six or seven occasions spread over two-plus years. The rest of the time, it doesn't strike you as being funny. You know it too well and you can very, very easily lose confidence in it. You have to think, "I trust that I thought this was funny eighteen months ago." You see what I mean? And there's a little bit inside you, kind of an almost muscular feeling, that tells you that the timing is right, whether the rhythms are right, whether the content is right. But it's always incredibly hard to know until an audience sees it.

And I think the extraordinarily helpful thing about writing comedy with someone else is that they react too. A lot of the time when I was writing with Graham Chapman, I always used to say that there were two types of days with Graham Chapman: there were the days when I did 80 percent of the work and there were the days when Graham did 2 percent of the work. But the extraordinary thing about him, he was the greatest sounding board I've ever come across, and if Graham laughed, I knew the audience would think it was funny. I think that's why comedy writers hunt in pairs.

GOLDMAN: I think comedy is the hardest thing there is. What is Henry Irving's great line? "Dying is easy. Comedy is hard." I don't know how people do it. You have a mind-set that goes a certain way. I don't have that.

CLEESE: You did at least two: *The Hot Rock* and *The Princess Bride*.

GOLDMAN: Very often in Hollywood they have seven or eight people in a television studio, writers all throwing in things. I think because they want to get as much help as they can. It's a difficult thing.

Who do you think is funny today? Who are your favorite comics? Yell out a name.

STUDENT: Dave Barry.

STUDENT: Robin Williams.

STUDENT: Eddie Izzard.

GOLDMAN: Do you realize how different Dave Barry is from Eddie Izzard is from anyone else? I think Eddie Izzard is brilliant, but I don't know why he is funny. There's something about him. I think if another actor did it, it wouldn't be. I don't know. It's a difficult thing, comedy.

CLEESE: He's one of the few comics I've met who wasn't seething with resentment. He's a truly sweet man. A phenomenon.

I think it's very helpful when you're figuring out a story to bore your friends with it. If you start telling someone a story and boiling it right down, not giving the dialogue but just telling the story, every time you tell it, you learn something from the act of telling it. If you're aware of the person listening, it gives you an awareness of whether the story really works. And sometimes, suddenly you tell them a bit and you think, "Whoops, that doesn't work," and then you can go away and work on that. And then the next time you're telling it to someone and you get to that bit and actually that bit works quite well now, but then you hit something else further down the line and that doesn't work, that doesn't move forward, that doesn't tie together. So now you can start working on that.

GOLDMAN: I think one of the reasons you can do that is because of your acting background. I'm so fragile when something's forming, if I tell you something and you say, "What are we having for dinner?" I'm dead. I'm so defeated by it. For the most part, I never show anybody anything until it's done.

Can I bring up one thing? Sketch comedy, in England, where John is from, they did that a lot, they didn't have stand-up. Is that not correct?

CLEESE: That's right. We had a tradition like your vaudeville tradition. We called it "music hall." A comic would come out and do jokes, but they didn't do stand-up in the sense that I understand it, which is that the stand-up comedian has a kind of worldview and almost all of his act is somehow putting that worldview across. In other words, there's a certain coherence in the way that he puts his material together. The old British music hall comedians would just come out and tell gags. They could have switched the order of the gags around and no one would have noticed.

GOLDMAN: We do have sketch comedy: *Saturday Night Live* is sketch comedy. But mostly we have stand-up. So stand-up comedians are now stars and it's a job, like rock star, that didn't used to exist.

CLEESE: That's right, and I notice there seems to be a natural kind of progression. If you look, for example, at any of the *Saturday Night Live* crowd or any of the Second City crowd or Woody Allen, it's that you start with sketches because somehow they're more manageable. It's kind of easier to get a three-minute sketch right when you start and then, when you get into your thirties, you inevitably get attracted to trying to work on a longer format. It might be a half hour if you are in television or it might be ninety or a hundred minutes if you're in movies. It's a huge transition, from being able to do sketches to being able to do full-length movies; even doing a ninety-minute movie as opposed to thirty-minute television, it's not three times harder, it's like twenty-five times harder. It's something to do with physiology because, in a half-hour format, you can start fairly straight and for twenty-two minutes it can simply get funnier and funnier and funnier. But you try to do that in a movie and you just run out of steam.

GOLDMAN: People get exhausted.

CLEESE: When we made the first Monty Python film, we only shot sketches; it was called *And Now for Something Completely Different.* It's patchy but what we found was this: At the first test screening, the audience thought it was terrific and they fell about until they got to forty-five minutes in, and then . . . they stopped laughing. And then, in the last fifteen to twenty minutes, they came back again. So, we said, "Okay, that material isn't so strong from about forty-five minutes to about sixty-five." So we took that material and—since it was a sketch show the order didn't matter much—we put it at the front and the audience fell about it and we thought, "Great, we sold it." And they got to forty-five minutes and they stopped laughing again. And then we did it a third time; it was like a scientist who couldn't believe his own experiment, and again they laughed for forty-five minutes and they stopped laughing. And there's something strange about this. You *have* to have a *story*—a narrative to carry you past forty-five minutes. Bill, did you have an experience like this?

GOLDMAN: I think stories are miracles. I don't know why it works when it works. If we all did, we would all just tell wonderful stories.

There's a book I always talk about that is the most simple piece of storytelling, *The Little Engine That Could.* Somehow, in that little children's book, we all want the toys to get across the mountain. That's all we have to do: get people involved with wanting. *How* you get them to want the toys to get across the mountain is the mystery. I believe that's really all storytelling is, put it on its most primitive storytelling level.

But storytelling, remember, began in the caves. All we're trying to do with any of this stuff is get through the night. You want it to be as nice as you can make it because it's scary in the night. There are animals out there. They can munch on us.

The original title of my last book, *Which Lie Did I Tell?*, was *The Current Campfire*, which is a phrase Gloria Steinem used in my presence: "Storytellers have been getting us through the night for centuries. Hollywood is the current campfire." I thought, "Wow, what a neat title that is."

I think that's important. Your parents told you stories when you were little and you wanted to hear them: "Tell me the one about the so-and-so again, Daddy." I think if you don't have the audience caring, *wanting* the story, it doesn't matter how wonderful or what else it is. It doesn't matter how brilliant your writing style is, people are going to stop reading you or stop watching you. I think that's true.

CLEESE: Okay, I've got some good questions here. Bill, the first one: "How can you retain creative control?"

GOLDMAN: Don't write movies. One thing that is unusual about me is I'm just a screenwriter. I had all kinds of chances when I was in my hot streak to direct movies *if* I would write them, but the idea of directing a movie is hateful to me. You're dealing with actors, all that stuff. But you have no power as a screenwriter. You get paid for silence; that's the deal.

If you guys want to be novelists, you will control it. I don't mean to be crabby, but you're not going to make a lot of money—you're not going to be able to support a family as a novelist. John Grisham can, Stephen King can, maybe ten others in all of America. The rest, you can't. You teach, and that's not a terrible life.

The thing about the movie business is this: Hollywood has always seduced us into silence by overpaying us. The fact is, you have no control. No screenwriter has ever had control. If you want to become a writer-producer or a writer-director, it would be different.

The reason screenwriting is such a hot occupation now is it's the easiest way to get into movies. Everybody here in this room, you all got into Cornell. You all know the alphabet. That's all words are, so you can write a script. You don't know how to be a cinematographer. That's hard. You don't know how to be a film editor.

That's hard. David Lean became a director from editing. But for the most part, people become directors from screenwriting, and that's why it's a hot thing.

But even directors don't have total control. Essentially, in a movie, if I'm giving you $80 million to make a movie for my company, you don't have total control. So anybody who's as low on the food chain as a screenwriter would never have control.

CLEESE: I remember writing with Charlie Crichton, this wonderful old guy who directed *A Fish Called Wanda*. He started directing in 1946. He'd begun as an editor in 1932. It was a privilege working with that guy because, at one point, I was trying to keep three threads of the story going at the same time and I put it on the page, cutting: ABC, ABC, ABC. Charlie said to me, "You can't do that." And I said, "I can't do ABC, ABC?" He said, "No, no. You've got to go ABC, BC, AC. But you can't go ABC, ABC, ABC." I said, "All right. I understand. But why not?" And he said, "I don't know, but the man who used to edit the Mack Sennett comedies told me so."

It was an incredible sense of excitement to be able to reach back to somebody's experience, something like sixty years before. What Charlie dreaded most, because anything that directors dread has to be good, is the writer-producer, and you might just bear in mind that that's a possible combination.

I think Bill and I and Steve Martin are the only three people in films who never ever wanted to direct a movie. I'd rather work in a garage. I think the hours are better and you don't have all that pressure. Just remember, if you don't want to direct but you want to write and have some control, there is a creature called the writer-producer.

I have another question, Bill: "When you're writing, to what extent does market research, demographics, all that kind of stuff, affect any of the decisions you take when you're constructing the story?"

GOLDMAN: Well, I'm going to sound very virginal on this. I don't know what's going to work. Remember: nobody knows anything.

I've never taken a movie because I thought it was going to be commercial or uncommercial. All I ever worry about when I'm offered something is, "Can I make it play? Can I figure out a way to tell the story? Would I want to see this movie? Would I be excited or pleased or whatever it is by it?" If those answers are yes, then I'll say, "Yes, I'll try and write the movie for you." But if I were offered a movie about twelve people in their nineties dying of cancer, I would not do that movie because, first of all, it would be hard to cast. Second of all, do you want to see that? I don't care if Bergman did it at his peak; well, if Bergman did it, I would go.

CLEESE: It could be very funny.

GOLDMAN: It turned out, to my shock, that I am not a genre writer in movies, by which I mean, I don't like doing the same thing over and over. After *Butch Cassidy*, I was offered an amazing number of Westerns, and yet I didn't do another Western until I did *Maverick*. After *Marathon Man*, I was offered an amazing number of thrillers. I didn't want to do another. I want to keep doing different things because there are problems that each genre has, and when you are trying make the movie come alive in your head, you have to try and solve those problems as well as you can. Now, once I've solved the problems, I don't want to have to attack them again. I know how to do that. I would rather try something else.

On *A Bridge Too Far*, Richard Attenborough, who was a wonderful man, wanted to make a huge movie. He felt the movie couldn't be, total, less than three hours. Well, that was fascinating to me because the greatest director I've ever worked with, George Roy Hill, said: "If you can't tell your story in an hour-fifty, you'd better be David Lean." I believe that movies are wildly long now. *A Bridge Too Far* was fascinating for me because I got to try writing a three-hour movie. That means several climaxes, at different points. It means you have a different kind of build when you're telling your story than if you're doing a ninety-minute movie. I don't want to write another one, but that's why I took that job.

CLEESE: All right. The big question from our audience is this: How do they get from here to there?

GOLDMAN: Say that again.

CLEESE: People here, sitting here now, who want to get somewhere in the film business. What do they do?

GOLDMAN: You write an original screenplay. You write a lot of them because most of them are going to stink. No, no! I don't mean that you're not talented. What I mean is you have to learn how to do it. It's hard. It's not a craft you're brought up with. The reason an *original* screenplay is gold is you don't know what they want.

Right now, they want to make Tom Hanks and Tom Cruise and Julia Roberts. Trust me. Three years ago, they didn't want to make Julia Roberts. She was in *Mary Reilly*. It was over for her; now she's hot again. Tom Hanks is riding, I think, the most remarkable hot streak that I can think of. It's been seven years now. He's had nothing but giant hits.

CLEESE: When people are on a streak, as you said earlier, you think they're so hot that it could never stop. Like Costner or Harrison Ford. You always think these people are absolutely unstoppable. Then they have some terrible movie and the whole thing changes.

GOLDMAN: Harrison Ford, a terrific star, who I don't know, was famous for having one agent for thirty years, a woman, he was her only client. He just left her to go to an agency. Why? Because he was scared. Why? Because *Sabrina* sucked. Because *Six Days, Seven Nights* sucked. I don't think he would have left her if *What Lies Beneath* had opened because that's a big hit. But people get panicked out there because stardom goes away.

When I say that my phone didn't ring for five years, I mean that. From 1980 to 1985, no one in the movie business spoke to me. I've been hot again for the last decade, fifteen years. That's terrific. I probably won't be a leper again because I'll be dead first. But it will happen. It happens to everybody out there.

I remember not many years ago when somebody very powerful said to me that he thought Arnold Schwarzenegger was the biggest star in history. Well, he had four or five movies that were phenomenal hits, I mean worldwide, just amazing successes and it's over. Part of it's because he had a heart problem, part of it was he was in his fifties. We like our action stars with a little bounce in their step.

What you want to do is write original screenplays, and this is going to sound crabby: you had better give a shit. You'd better write something you believe you can make play; you want to write a story that you think you can make work. You think, "Wow, I love that." Whatever it is you think you can make *work*.

I was brought up in the '30s and '40s on certain kinds of genres. The first hit I had was Paul Newman in *Harper*. I loved Bogart, so that was the fuel, if you will, that made me do that. I loved Westerns so, when I wrote *Butch Cassidy*, I had all the Westerns that I loved as a kid when growing up that gave me an emotional power. It made me say, "I can do this. I love that, I can do this." So, you better not take a genre because it's hot. You better not write *Scream* right now. You better write something you care about, and an original screenplay is worth gold because you own it and that's how careers are made.

Frank Darabont wrote a great, great screenplay from a Stephen King book called *The Shawshank Redemption*, which is one of my favorite movies of the decade, and he was offered a great deal of money for the script. And he had no money and he said, "No, this is my shot. I want to direct this." He'd never directed and he got this shot and his career is now as hot as anybody. But all the power was in the script. The script is everything *until* you sell it. Then you begin to get into other problems. So the first thing I would do is, I would think about what kind of movies do I really love? If you were on a desert island, what would be the half-dozen movies you would have to take with you? Figure out what appeals to you and try and write that. And it may stink, but then you write another one and, in theory, you'll learn more and maybe you'll get lucky. But I think that's the way to get in the movie business.

CLEESE: The other absolutely great thing about starting a screenplay is that the moment that you sit down and you start trying to write your first screenplay, you start learning from the movies that you watch because, in the act of writing your own screenplay, you start priming your own mind with questions about how to do this and how to do that, and that's when you start *learning*.

GOLDMAN: I remember once, a few years ago, I was doing something—I can't think of what now—and I thought, "How did Lean and Bolt do it in *Lawrence?*" So I called up my video store and I rented *Lawrence of Arabia*, and I went over and over and over this sequence to see how they did it because it moved me and I thought, "Oh, they went here and then there, and then there." So you'll find you don't look at movies the way you used to.

It's a different world but you have to take it seriously and *learn* about it. You just do. You learn about writing, I think, by writing. It helps to read screenplays, see how various writers do it.

Bob Towne wrote a great screenplay for *Chinatown*. Read *Chinatown*, see how he did it. Some of the greatest scenes ever written in movies are in *Chinatown*. The "she's my daughter/she's my sister" scene—how did he write that? Well, figure it out. Read what goes before and read what comes after—how did he set it up, and then, wow, it happens. You might be able to do that if you really work at it.

CLEESE: Remember what Bill was saying about going and watching a movie three times in a row. Well, after you've begun to write your first screenplay, if you start watching a new movie and it's good, you're still what we call in England a *punter*. If it's really good, you just sit there and you're in it and you're not analyzing it because it's got you. It's only when something goes wrong and you say, "Hmm, I don't think much of that." That's when you start analyzing. You see, if the movie's *got* you, you're just a member of the audience having a wonderful time. That's why, to learn, you have to watch a really good movie several times, till you're not *in* it. I had been writing eight or nine years before I started a screenplay because

I was perfectly happy doing sketches. But then, when I started on movies, I just could not figure out how to do what I call "time sequences," you know, how to do things in what order, and how to indicate whether any period of time has passed. Do I have to indicate to the audience that this scene is two weeks later as opposed to two hours later? And I realized that, although I'd been writing for seven or eight years, I had no idea how to solve that. Then I started watching movies differently and a few months later, I basically got it. Answer: most of the time you don't have to explain how much time has passed. One of the problems in *A Fish Called Wanda* was the long time it would take getting the guy to trial. So we just kind of never mentioned this, and nobody said, "Well, that happened a bit quick, didn't it?"

Now, there's a question here I thought was very interesting: Someone asks, "What other classes should these students be taking that would help the writing, other than the obvious ones?"

GOLDMAN: Well, I believe this: you're going to look at a lot of movies—you have to—and the most important moment for you is when you say, "Wait a minute, why am I bored?"

When I first heard of film schools, I thought, "What's the punch line?" The idea of going to school for movies, that's not what you did back then. Now that's what everybody does. But the problem with a lot of film school kids is all they know are other movies. They know the first eleven shots of Kurosawa's *Yojimbo*, but that's *all* they know, and the problem is their work becomes like the gooney gooney bird that flies in increasingly smaller circles so it ends up swallowed up by its own asshole. I think what happens with a lot of these guys is that their movies only have references to other movies. I think most of the famous film figures out there have never read a book. That doesn't mean they aren't greatly gifted at what they do. But just take the giants out there—I bet you George Lucas and Steven Spielberg and James Cameron, greatly gifted people, don't have piles of books by their bedside.

STUDENT: It shows.

GOLDMAN: I think it shows too, but that's just my particular taste; they're fabulous entertainers, but it's limited. The fact is, the more you know, the better off you are.

CLEESE: When Louis Malle finished making a movie, the moment he'd edited it, he would go back to the place where he had a house in France, which was a small town in western France, and he would just sit around there and, you know, have coffee in the marketplace and talk to everyone and kind of go into a decompression chamber to get out of movies. And later he'd slowly start looking around to see what he was going to do next. And I remember he joked about Truffaut—Truffaut made a great movie called *La nuit américaine*, called *Day for Night* here, about a crew making a movie. And Malle said, "Truffaut made that movie because he doesn't know about anything else now. All he does is make movies, and so he has to make movies about making movies."

One of the things that worries me, one of the trends in America now, is that so many movies are actually about the entertainment business. I think that the most exciting movies are the movies that take something about life, real life, that I haven't noticed, present or past or future, and put that on film. That's what excites me.

Here's another question: What can you say about dialogue, Bill? You've got an ear for it.

GOLDMAN: It doesn't matter in a movie as much as it does in almost any art form that I can think of because we can only quote, "Frankly, my dear, I don't give a damn," and maybe half a dozen other lines from movies. The reason we can't quote more is that the dialogue doesn't matter. It's the whole movie that matters. In other words, it's the whole visual that you see as well as the dialogue. I'm not talking about comedy because in comedy, the dialogue is everything. But in most movies, the dialogue is not important. If it gets where you're going, it's done its job. If you're going to do *All about Eve* like Mr. Mankiewicz did, it's nice to be brilliant. But, for the most part, movies don't require brilliant dialogue. It just has to be solid and tell the story. Movies are not about dialogue. It's one of the great myths. Screenwriting is not about dialogue.

CLEESE: I think you can say there are really two separate categories in comedy. In one, there are lots of gags, wisecracks, or one-liners that you could quote to someone and they'd be funny out of context. But the kind of comedy that, by and large, I prefer is where the situation itself is funny. Some character has got himself in an awfully embarrassing situation and he has to try and get out of it and, of course, what he does to get out of it lands him in an even worse situation. I love that kind of writing. But there, if the situation is funny, you don't really need funny lines.

One of the problems with a lot of comedy that is written is that people write stories that could be dramas and then try and put jokes into them. So be very, very painstaking when you're constructing comedies. Create funny situations, which will take much, much longer. But your reward is that the dialogue comes so easily because the situation's funny. When I did *Fawlty Towers* with my first wife, Connie Booth, we used to spend two to two-and-a-half weeks coming up with the stories for those episodes, and then we could write them easily in a week or ten days because once we had the situations, then the lines followed.

Let's have a few questions now.

STUDENT: Mr. Goldman, you cautioned about reading too much literature, but I got a lot more out of *Life of Brian* knowing a little bit about the Bible and having a certain knowledge and background, which I think is useful in writing and viewing other work.

GOLDMAN: Yes, you should do as much reading as you can do. You're not going to use it all, but you should read. Basically, it grounds you, I think. What you write, the snowball you roll down the hill which gathers weight, will gather more weight if you're not a simpleton.

The other thing I was going to say is, you're all sitting around a lot. Why don't you rent a movie and look at it with a couple of friends and talk about it afterwards and say, "Why did that suck, and why was that good, or was the whole movie good, or did the whole movie suck?" Seriously, not like a critic, not thumbs up, thumbs down, but how would you fix it?

When I doctor movies, which I do, it has all to do with craft. It does not have to do with, do I love this material? It has to do with, can I bring this dying beast back to life? And sometimes you can and sometimes you can't. I doctored a movie—it was a great failure for Attenborough called *Chaplin.* It had some terrific stuff in it, a wonderful performance by Robert Downey. I felt the problem was Chaplin had a horrible childhood, Dickensian, and at the end of the movie when he was in his seventies, he was accepted back into Hollywood and won an Oscar. If anybody saw that footage of this old, old man sobbing in a wheelchair, it was very, very effective. Chaplin was a music hall comic. He came to America, very strange man sexually, he had a terrible life, he committed his mother to an insane asylum (not a happy day). One day he went into a prop house in California and he came out with the most famous single image in world movies: the tramp. He had the walk, he had the cane, he had the hat. Suddenly, this thing happened, and I wanted to end the movie at that moment, just as he was walking in that tramp persona back to the set, because I thought, after that, his life was just, "Well, I had this hit, and then I had that hit, and then I got more famous and I knocked up this girl, et cetera, et cetera." Attenborough wanted them both, and I think that's, for me, what killed the movie. It was people saying things like, "John Cleese, I haven't seen you for seventeen years since the dance at Sir Cedric's," things they wouldn't actually say to convey the passage of time. Anyway, I couldn't help on that. The movie did not work.

A movie I doctored that was a huge success was *Twins,* which was Schwarzenegger and DeVito, and it's about these twins who are trying to find their mother. When I came on the movie, the mother was dead. Essentially, what I did was convince Reitman, the director, that if she's dead, there's no movie. She's got to be alive and they've got to try and find her. I'm not saying that that made the movie work—we don't know what made the movie work—but it was a gigantic hit. What you do when you doctor is try and figure out what's wrong here, what's bearable, what you can try and make work. You try to get rid of the awfulness. And sometimes you can and sometimes you can't.

CLEESE: I love these examples.

GOLDMAN: Well, I had a bizarre experience. About a year and a half ago, I was sent a script called *The Hollow Man* that Paul Verhoeven was going to direct. Verhoeven has had a strange career. *Showgirls* didn't help. So, I read the script and I thought, "It's a really terrible script." But I thought if the special effects worked, it could be a very, very exciting and different movie, and I'd never done special effects so I thought that could be interesting. So, I go out to meet with Verhoeven and we're talking, and I say, "Well, the first scene I would change is, I don't like that scene there." And he said, "Oh, I love that scene, that's my favorite scene in the movie." I said, "Okay, we'll leave that." And then I went to what I thought was the next awful thing, and he said, "Oh, that's wonderful stuff." We talked for about an hour and I said, "Paul, you love this script." And he said, "Yes, I do." And I said, "Then, why am I here?" And he said, "I don't want you here. The studio wants somebody to make it better, but I'm going to shoot what I have." So, basically, I started rewriting for a director, knowing he wouldn't like anything that I was rewriting. I haven't seen the movie, but I gather it sucks although the special effects are terrific. I'll never know if it could have been saved. That's the thing: you never know. He might have been right; he might have been wrong. It's one of those things.

I was the original writer on the last *Mission: Impossible*. All that's left of mine is the climax. If you've seen it, the climax is the climbing up the rocks sequence. I couldn't come up with a good villain and Bob Towne did. It's very hard, now that Communism has fallen, to come up with a good villain. I'm serious. It's horrible for screenwriters.

I doctored *Indecent Proposal*, which was a huge hit. When I came on, John Cusack had turned it down. They couldn't get anyone to do it. I wrote a draft and I don't think they changed anything. I don't know why the actors decided to do it or didn't do it, but it was an enormous success so that's good for me. But ultimately, when you doctor, you're trying to figure out what's keepable here—what was the thing that they thought they were making in the beginning—'cause usually what happens is this:

A great cinematographer, Gordon Willis (*The Godfather I* and *II* and a lot of Woody Allen's), said to me in an interview I was doing with him that his great skill is not lighting; his great skill is that he remembers where we were going before we started shooting. I'll try and explain. A movie is a huge number of people and tremendous pressure and tremendous money being spent, and the director is being eaten alive because the star won't come out of her trailer and the studio is screaming at him that he's a half a day behind.

We're telling the story, but things start to happen on set. Suddenly, some kid will give a terrific little scene and they'll say, "He's good. I want to see more of that kid." And suddenly the story gets lost, and you can't ever get it back. Willis would say, "This is not the movie we said we were going to make." And that's a great strength because it's chaos on a movie set.

CLEESE: When you're writing, you sometimes pin up in front of you a key word just to make sure you don't forget where you're trying to get to.

GOLDMAN: Yes, one other thing that I do, I meant to tell you this, I tend to write for dead actors. When I am writing a movie, there are certain people who I revere: Jimmy Cagney, Cary Grant, et cetera. And I'll think, "Shit, if I had Cary Grant in this part, this scene would be so charming. How can I make this work for Cary Grant?" I do that a lot. I don't write for Dustin Hoffman. I write for those people, like Katherine Hepburn, who no longer work, but who were part of my childhood. It gives you a fix on the character you're writing.

CLEESE: Charlie Crichton said that at the Ealing Studios they'd picture a living actor while writing, but then cast someone else! Let me explain my own experience. When you're trying to imagine a new character, obviously you can base it on someone that you know, and also we all have inside ourselves kind of different facets of our own character, and it may be that one of those is suitable and you can find that person within yourself when you're writing. It's a strange process and I think this is what actors do as they build a character. At the beginning, you don't know what is quite appropriate for the character that you're playing, and then you do something and it feels right. It just feels right, and you kind of remember that, and then you're trying to find the voice and you say a sentence and it just, yeah . . . I like the way it sounded when I said that sentence. And then you do a gesture and that feels right too, and ever so slowly you begin to assemble this character and it's as though it's inside you somewhere. At the beginning, it's a very, very, very slow process because you're not quite sure if something's right, and maybe it is and you incorporate it and then the next day it doesn't feel quite right and you take it out again. But after a time, you have enough of these characteristics within you, not just the voice but the gestures, the movements and everything, and you start pulling it all together. Novelists, in particular, have said there's a very, very exciting moment when suddenly one of your characters starts taking over from you and kind of writing itself. Right?

GOLDMAN: It's true. When they start talking, it's wonderful. But you can't make them do that.

Let me talk very briefly about the nuts and bolts of doing all this. Look, you have full lives, you're trying to get laid, you're trying to graduate, you're trying to do all kinds of things, right? There's not a lot of time in the day. When you write, you have to have a schedule that works for you, and you must protect it to the *death*. If you could only write two mornings a week, then you must protect from seven to eight on Tuesdays and Fridays. Those must be your hours and you must be at your pad or at your computer or your typewriter or whatever it is. Nothing may happen, but you've got to be there.

When I was a kid, in my terrible years, when I said I wanted to be a writer, people would say, "What do you want to do next?" Meaning it wasn't a real occupation like being a doctor or a lawyer. Those are real occupations.

Being a writer, nobody cares if I live or die. Until I finish something, it's nothing. So, I think if you don't protect your time, you have almost no chance. I don't care if it's only two hours a week, you'd better save those two hours.

In writing a movie, once I actually start to write, I try to write the first day—this is very mechanical but it helps me—three pages. Now, three pages of a novel is tough. A movie, you write, "FADE IN," in caps; double space; "A classroom at Cornell"; double space; "Bill and John are speaking to students"; double space; "Bill is sixty-so-and-so, John is . . ." Well, you've got half a page and you haven't started yet—it's wonderful. I mean that. So I try and not quit the first day, and I'll come back and fix it, all right, but I want to get three pages. If you can't write that much, write one page.

I believe movies should be written with speed. When you're writing a movie, turn out a lot. If you're somebody for whom one page is the maximum, make sure you do the one page. You have to go forward because the minute you are two days in the same space, the demons will come along and say: "Well, this sucks. You have no talent." The minute you let that voice get control of you, you're in trouble.

CLEESE: Which is why, I think, you can hurt yourself by reading too much literature. Because then you write a sentence and you think, "Well, that's Thomas Hardy, isn't it?" You write something else and, "That's sort of Henry James." You know, you become very self-conscious, which kills anything creative.

I think the most important things, as Bill suggested, is to set aside times in your week when all you're going to do is *write*. Because any time you leave your diary blank, it'll fill itself up. So, what you want to do is to figure out when you can write for, I think, an hour and a half because less doesn't really work, as we'll see when we talk more about the creative process. Write that in your calendar twice a week, say, and *stick* to it. And if you have to cancel it, put it in somewhere else because it's the writing time that will always get squeezed, and that's because writing is really hard work and you know how we all shy away from real thinking. Any excuse—you'll sit down to write and suddenly you'll realize you've not washed your socks or that that shelf is crooked and you really can't quite start until you've straightened it. Robert Benchley wrote a whole funny piece about this. So you've got to give yourself creative space and make it absolutely regular. That's where the discipline comes in, as Bill says.

Let's talk about the creative process.

GOLDMAN: Okay.

CLEESE: When you get up in the morning and you're going to write, how long does it take before you start typing?

GOLDMAN: Everybody has different work habits. For me, the novelist of the century was Graham Greene. Graham Greene wrote three hundred words every day of his life, and he counted them and at the end of the three hundredth word—he could be in the middle of a sentence—he stopped. That was his rhythm. That worked for him.

There's no right way of doing it. I know we all have trouble starting in the morning. I know a young writer, she's very good, who says she has no trouble writing! Her problem is sitting down to do it because getting to her computer is a minefield. She has a baby, that has to be done; she has a husband, his laundry has to be done; she has all these things that stop her and suddenly it's four p.m. and there's no point in starting at four p.m. and another day is gone. She can do that for weeks.

CLEESE: An English writer I admire, Denis Norden, told me, "Never underestimate the excuses that your unconscious will come up with."

GOLDMAN: If you're just pulling something out of yourself, there's nothing that makes you do it but your own need to get that down, and that's why I said you'd better give a shit. You'd better want the story you're telling to be a story that interests you. It only has to interest you.

And the other thing—you've got to protect time. My first and greatest editor, Hiram Haydn, had four kids and ran a publishing house, and he was a novelist and his only time to write was Sunday mornings. He would write from seven to eleven every Sunday morning.

He didn't like to do that, but that's the only time he had available to him and that was *sacred*. The kids knew it, his wife knew it, nobody could go near him for those four hours and he actually was able to write novels that way.

Four hours a week, if you really want to do this for your life, is not that big a deal, folks, but you've got to do it. I don't think you should tell people about it because most of what we do isn't going to be any good; most of it won't get published; most of it won't get made into movies.

CLEESE: The wonderful thing is you can rewrite.

GOLDMAN: Yes.

CLEESE: *A Fish Called Wanda* took me thirteen drafts, six major and seven minor redrafts. But, Bill, you don't rewrite as much as most people.

GOLDMAN: No, I don't, because I'm not good at it. Basically, I spend so long getting ready and I never start until I have those words in front of me and, if I've made a major mistake in those words, if the story is screwed up and corkscrewing on me, I'll have to stop and go back to the top and try and figure out what I did wrong. But for the most part, my time is taken at the start, building up confidence and, again, trying to figure out which story I want to tell.

I had a terrific movie, I think, *All the President's Men*. It's the Woodward and Bernstein Watergate story, and the middle of the book tells how they made a mistake and almost cost everyone their jobs, et cetera, et cetera. I ended the movie on that mistake! The logic being that they were media darlings—everybody knew that they were eventually proved right—and so I only told half the story of their book and we got great, great praise for how authentic and accurate we were. I wasn't accurate at all. I was accurate about the tone of what we were doing. I didn't "Hollywood" it up. The studios are always saying, "Well can't there be a love affair, can't there be this, can't we have more action?"

One of the things that's happening now, which is new, is the studios have development people. I am working with Dick Donner and Mel Gibson on *Maverick*. Now, they've both directed, Gibson won an Oscar—I mean they're really not dumb guys, right? And there are these three gnomes from Warner Brothers who are sitting in a room with us taking notes, and then I would get notes at the end of a week saying: "We feel the movie would be better if it was funnier and more exciting." And I said, "Fuck you." I feel the same thing. If I could make it funnier and more exciting, I would. Do you think I'm sitting there and saying, "This could be so funny, but I can't be bothered"?

CLEESE: Yes?

STUDENT: I notice on action films and a lot of the time on different movies there always is an arsenal of writers who have gone over and over the script and it's still bad.

GOLDMAN: Why do you think that is?

STUDENT: It seems as though the studios want something specific and the writers are trying to get at that.

GOLDMAN: Sometimes it's that. But an amazing amount of the time it's because of a movie star's ego. Most movies, except for action pictures, are a boy and a girl. Well, the girl is always going to think the guy's part is better so she's going to say, "Well, I want a writer to come in and help the movie, but maybe make my part so I understand it better." And the studio is going to say, "Damn, we're going to have to pay $300,000 to this putz writer, but we'll do it to keep her happy." And then the guy is going to say this: "Whoa, where did my part go?" So one of the things that happens is you get a lot of writers in to please people's egos along with the directors and the producers. A lot of it's that. It's always kind of been thus, but the reason you see many more names now is because it used to not matter. Today, with cassettes and DVDs, if a movie's a hit, it could matter tens and hundreds of thousands of dollars if a writer gets billing. So everybody now wants billing on a movie because if the movie works, and nobody knows anything and it might, there's a huge amount of money that's coming to you.

I always wish we could change directors. I always say, "Well this guy is terrific on people in a room but he stinks when it comes to size, so let's bring in another director for the big stuff." They say you can't do that.

But stars want everything, and one of the things you know when you're writing the script is, if you write a good line at the end of a scene and the secondary performer has that good line, *don't do that*! Rewrite the scene so the star has that good line.

Stars, basically, are very shrewd and, except for Jodie Foster, not particularly educated. I mean that. John Travolta is a wonderful performer, but he didn't go to Harvard. He was working when he was seventeen—most of them were working when they were seventeen. They want to be on Broadway, Off Broadway, on television. Leonardo DiCaprio's been working since he was two. Jodie Foster, who also started working when she was two, went to Yale and has a brilliant academic mind. She's the only one I've ever met in thirty-five years who is just brilliant, not just shrewd—they're all shrewd and smart and deadly, but Jodie Foster is really something different.

CLEESE: Most actors, not all in my experience, are really only thinking about their own part. It doesn't necessarily mean that they're being selfish, but they're just looking at it through the lens of their own part.

Basically, any project has got to have one organizing intelligence. Now, if that organizing intelligence is any good, it's listening to a lot of people but, ultimately, it's making up its mind which bits of advice it's going to listen to and which it's going to ignore. And I think that if you have a lot of writers, it's almost certainly a sign there isn't one organizing intelligence. There are a lot of people in there, and the people in charge don't really agree, and don't really know what they want. I think it's a sign of a disaster.

GOLDMAN: One of the things you have to realize, if you really want to write movies and you really want somebody to make your movie, you're going to have to deal with the reality of the movie star. Know this about them: they're all charming, they're all bright, they're all clever. They were not born that way. One of the reasons they get divorced when they make it big is because the first wife remembers what a klutz he was and says, "Hey, take out the garbage."

When you become a star, everybody says, "Oh, you're so wonderful." I've been with stars where somebody will say, "My God, that watch. What is that watch? Where did you get that watch? It's the most beautiful watch. It's the most beautiful style." And the star begins to think, "I have really great taste in watches!"

I wrote once, "Barbra Streisand gets up and goes to bed and never has a single human being disagree with her." Now, that eats away at your soul.

Stars all know they're not going to stay close to the fire forever, and it's not just the $20 million, which is nice, thank you very much, it's all of the accoutrements. It's about being able to say, "God, I want to go to Acapulco; if only there was a jet I could take." Boom! "Guess what, Tommy, I'll get you a jet. It's there when you want it, twenty-four hours." One of the star perks now which I know of, a star has a limo and driver twenty-four hours a day. Fine, standard, they all have that. But he also has a sports car and sports car driver twenty-four hours a day. Why? Because sometimes, he doesn't know when, he might like to drive the sports car. So, when he's driving along in the limo with the sports car following, sometimes he'll stop, he gets in the sports car, the sports car driver will get in the limousine, the star will go tooling along in the sports car. When he gets bored, he will get back in the limousine. That costs a lot of money. Guess what: studios will say, "Oh, we love it that you would have a sports car twenty-four hours a day. What's a couple of hundred thousand dollars?" There's a wonderful phrase I used in *Adventures in the Screen Trade* told me by a great producer: "Add one-third for the shit." That's a line about stars. If you're going to have a star, he's going to cost you: their own hairdressers, their own waiter, their own this, their own that. It's not terrific, but if it's what makes them happy, when they are in power, they can get that.

So you'd better write for them. Remember this: stars have no flaws. I've written this and written this. They are perfect. A star will not play flawed. They *will not* play flawed.

A great movie story: We all know *Lord Jim*, a wonderful Conrad novel about a man who commits an act of cowardice and then spends the rest of his life atoning for it. Well, no one would play the lead, so they made a movie about a guy who didn't commit an act of cowardice and spent the rest of his life atoning for it.

Stars will not play flawed. You'd better make them perfect. If they fail, there's a reason—they want their kid to be stronger so they might fail and wink at the audience. Know this: you'd better write perfect parts for perfect people. That's the deal, folks, alas.

STUDENT: What about the movie rating system and censorship? I was thinking about *The Last Temptation of Christ* and the censorship that followed its release.

GOLDMAN: That was very controversial. A lot of people were upset about that movie.

CLEESE: Bill, have you ever been on a movie where people say, "We don't want to make a movie about that subject," on the grounds of taste?

GOLDMAN: No, never. Studios spend money to get these things going. When I say movies are very slow, usually it starts with a producer who options a piece of material, then he looks for a studio. He usually doesn't take an option with his own money, so he needs the studio's money; he's got to find a studio who will give him the money, *then* he tries to find a writer—that's six months of his life. It's very slow, so if there's trouble, it would happen before I get brought in. The studio would say, "I don't want to do that movie." Once you get geared up, it wouldn't happen.

STUDENT: You were going to talk about writing *The Princess Bride*.

GOLDMAN: Well, I was going to talk about it in the sense of not knowing what I'm doing. I have always loved the kind of stuff that *The Princess Bride* is, yet I didn't know how to do it— the novel, that is.

So I wrote the opening chapter in the book, which essentially is how Buttercup became the most beautiful woman in the world, and that was, I don't know, fifteen or twenty pages. And then I wrote the second chapter about Prince Humperdinck, who's killing an ape or something, which is short, about five pages. Then I was dry. I had all these stories in my head like the Cliffs of Insanity, the climb up the Cliffs, and the Zoo of Death. I had all this stuff. I had these people and I didn't know how to get there, and for weeks I was storming around trying to figure out what to do because it was closing. I could sense it fading, the whole story, so that in a year you would say, "Why did you want to write that? What was that about? It's stupid." And then one day I was walking along in New York and it dropped into my head: what if I was writing an abridgement of an earlier novel and I was just going to show the good parts of the earlier novel? And once I had that realization, I had the only fabulous writing experience of my life. I didn't know what I was doing. I was showing it to my wife then, and I would say, "What is this?" And she'd say, "I don't know, but keep going." It was this amazing emotional thing for me and I don't know why.

I will tell you this, the high point of my writing life, I was walking to my office and Wesley was in the machine and he was being tortured and I was wondering how I was going to get him out, and I'm walking up and I had my coffee and I was sitting at my desk and I remember writing: "Wesley lay dead by the machine." I'd killed him and I thought, "Jesus, what did you do?" And I suddenly burst into hysterical tears out of nowhere and I ran to the bathroom and ran water over my face, and I looked up and saw my face in the mirror—this anguished, red face—and I thought, "Who are you and where are we?" I didn't know. It was just this strange emotional outpouring for me. And then I just wrote the rest of the book. It was the most wonderful releasing thing. I really felt on top of my material; I knew where it was going, I loved the people. I had no idea what it was, but I had this thing and I don't know . . . if I hadn't gotten that idea of the abridgement, would I ever have written it.

But when you write, there is a pulse. Suddenly I want to tell something, and I want to tell it now. Then you must go to your office because if you don't tell it now, it will leave you. You think it will come back later but it never does. I don't know about you, but with me, it never does. You have to grab onto it because there are very few times in your career—I hope you all have wonderful careers—when you're right on top of your material and you'll feel this wonderful sense of, "Yes, I'm terrific. Look at this. Look what I can do." It's marvelous but it doesn't happen much. You've got to basically go with it when you can because it disappears, it goes away. It does for me, anyway.

STUDENT: You both wrote before computers. Did computers change the creative writing process?

GOLDMAN: It doesn't make you any better; it just makes you faster and you lose more. I lose stuff all the time if I forget to save. It's faster, it *is* faster. I don't think it has anything to do with the writing. I would guess that people were better when they used quill pens because you'd pause more over each word: what is the potency of this word, and do I want to have this sentence?

STUDENT: Would you ever write a bloodbath movie?

GOLDMAN: I loved *The Matrix*, but if you said to me, "Will you write *The Matrix*?" I would say, "I don't know how to do that." It's not something I do. I have an emotional block, or whatever I'm trying to say, toward that kind of stuff. John can write farce. I have no ability at farce. John takes farce very seriously. Don't you?

CLEESE: It has to be. If you play it in a different way, it could be tragedy. Poor, poor Basil Fawlty, how *awful* for him. . . .

STUDENT: You were talking about writing for specific people who wouldn't actually be in the movie but are characterizations of the kind of actors who motivate you. When you're writing, do you first compose a cast of characters for what story they have to tell or come up with personalities that would be best in getting the story across?

CLEESE: I think that the hardest thing in the world is to hold plot and character in your mind at the same time. I find it very, very hard to do. What I tend to do is kind of oscillate between the two.

GOLDMAN: Stories are what grab me first. That's what I gravitate toward. I never think, "Oh, look at that old guy in the wheelchair playing tennis. I'll write a book about him." That's not the way my head works.

CLEESE: I wanted to say one thing about plot. It's not so much about character, but my experience of story is that you've very often got what you need there already. I think when people feel that they're stuck on plot, they think somehow they have to bring in something new from *outside*. Whereas, I think the most useful thing you can do is look very, very carefully at what you've got and ask the most prosaic of questions, which is, what do these characters need to do in this situation? For example, writing *A Fish Called Wanda*, I could not figure out what to do with Michael Palin in the middle of the movie. I knew he was in at the beginning of the movie and I knew he was very funny at the end of the movie. Meanwhile, Jamie's trying to get the locket back from me and Kevin is jealously stalking us. But I didn't know what to do with Michael. And it's extraordinary when you think the biggest laughs in the movie are actually him killing the dogs by accident. Well, that's the *last* bit of the movie that I wrote. I just asked myself, "What would he be doing?" He would be trying to help the gang boss. How would he be trying to help the gang boss? There was only one witness; he would be trying to kill the witness. But he keeps missing. So, it was all there but I'd been looking outside.

GOLDMAN: I would say this: if any of you, when you get stuck, if you can find a reader, they're worth gold. By a reader I mean someone who knows what they are talking about and will tell you the truth! Because it's easier to say, "Oh, it's great, Bill." That's easy. But, what's hard is to say, "This isn't right," because I'm liable to say you don't care for me, goodbye. So, if you can find someone whose taste you approve of and like, who you can give something you've written who will say, "No, you've got to make this better," and you can still keep the friendship, that's worth gold. It's very hard for everybody to make that work because it's very risky for the other person. When I read stuff by young writers, which I do a lot, I always say, "Do you want me to be honest or do you want me to tell you you're wonderful?" And they all say, "I just want your honesty." And I'll say, "Fine." And I always start with a scene and I'll say, "Well, I'm curious about why you wrote this." And he'll say, "Oh, I love that scene." It's like the experience with Paul Verhoeven, and then you know they don't want to hear anything except that they're wonderful and that's what you must tell them. I've always been pretty good, for someone who's nuts, in accepting criticism because we all get stuck, don't we, all the time, and if someone can tell you what's wrong, it's gold for you. One of the reasons why I think it's great to write with someone else is you've got another mind saying, "What if we go there?" which I would never have thought of. Anyway, a reader is someone who is very valuable and who will actually tell you the truth, and who you'll listen to and not get angry at.

CLEESE: The wonderful thing about having a cowriter is that the two of you become an animal that is not either of you and which will get you to places that you would never ever get to on your own. I find that exciting.

When Bill was talking about getting on a purple streak when he was writing *The Princess Bride*, I suddenly thought, we need to talk about the bad times too, because there are times when you do get really stuck, as Bill mentioned. I was once told something which has helped me ever since. There was this guy called Gregory Bateson—he was an extraordinary brilliant man. I don't know what you call him—a biologist or philosopher. He was married to Margaret Mead. And Bateson said, "You can't have a new idea until you've gotten rid of an old one." And sometimes when you get really stuck, just bear that in mind because maybe what you are doing, being stuck, is kind of clearing a space for a new idea to come in.

I'll give you another thought from Robin Skynner, the guy I wrote the two psychology books with. He said, "When you get stuck writing, it's part of the process. You can't write and not be stuck some of the time. Otherwise, it's like saying that, when you eat a meal, it's really good when the fork is moving towards your mouth with the food on it, and kind of bad and negative and a waste of time when the fork's moving back empty." If you think of that, that's what writing is about. Sometimes it's coming, and sometimes it isn't, but it's all part of the same process and you just have to be patient.

GOLDMAN: Tennessee Williams said, "There are three or four days when the play opens itself to me." And the bulk of the quality of whatever play he was writing, whether it was *A Streetcar Named Desire* or *The Glass Menagerie* or *Cat on a Hot Tin Roof*, whatever it was, the bulk of the quality of those plays came in those three or four days. The rest of it is anguish when you sit there and you know it's just toothpaste. It's not like you wake up and say, "I want to have a really rotten day today. I want to just feel like a failure all day long, that's for me!" It just happens. It just is part of the deal.

CLEESE: Well, we're now coming up towards the end of our third hour and I can tell our energy's dropping a little bit and people quite justifiably are fiddling and we're rambling on and on. Let's have any last questions.

STUDENT: I'm interested in something you brought up earlier about the process of adapting a book to a screenplay, particularly in terms of *The Princess Bride*, because you wrote both. How did you decide what to keep and what to change from the original story?

GOLDMAN: It was a thirteen-year nightmare. I wrote the first draft, Fox optioned the book but they didn't know if it was a movie, so they owned the book but I owned the screenplay. There was a director who was very hot then named Richard Lester, who directed the Beatles films. Lester was sent my screenplay, loved it, I worked with him for a little bit, we were all set to go, when the studio head who had bought the movie was fired, so that meant the movie was put into the icebox: it would never happen. Finally, after several years, because when I wrote the book I hadn't realized how much it would come to mean to me, I did something remarkable. I bought it back with my own money. I didn't have another deal; I just bought it back and I owned it. And for years it was a cursed project—for *years*. I had two studios that went bust when they were going to make it and then, finally, Rob Reiner came on board but we didn't have enough money. In other words, when I wrote the script, the whole sequence of the Zoo of Death, we couldn't afford it. We couldn't afford monsters. We couldn't afford all kinds of stuff. So we basically made the movie. It's amazing because it's a special effects movie, we made it for $15 million, which would be $30 million today, which is still low because the average Hollywood movie now is $60 million. But basically, a lot of what happened in that movie and that script is because we didn't have any money. We couldn't be grand. I like the movie, but there were other things I would have wished for and I'm sure Reiner would have wished other things too.

The fact is, you are always at the mercy of how much money you have. You don't want to hear about money but a studio is going to say, "Here's what we'll give you, we'll give you *x* and you make the movie and you'll have forty-four days and that's all." And if you really want to make it, you sign on. And *that's* what you make it on. And if you go over budget and the movie's a hit, you're okay. If you go over budget and the movie is a stiff, your career is grievously wounded.

CLEESE: Last question.

STUDENT: From what I've read, it seems, in the movie business, that the power has shifted from when it first started, when it was the studios. Then around in the '50s the directors took over, and then it was agents, and then actors. Who do you think is going to be next in terms of power? Do you think writers will have more power?

GOLDMAN: Alas, I wish we did, but we won't have it. One thing you must understand is agents have no power. Agents are at the mercy of the stars they have. When a star leaves, the agent is wounded. Agents can't do very much, they just live long because they have no emotions. They have no power. It's always been the same thing: the studio has power, directors have power, stars have power, writers *don't* have power. And a lot of what you see—the way you see—a lot of what you see is that power. In other words, stars will affect movies and directors.

CLEESE: Let me add one thing. I should have said this earlier, about television. The two best-organized shows I ever did were *Cheers* and *Third Rock from the Sun*. Everybody there was a producer *and* a writer. And that's what you can find in television. You can find these congregations of writers who've been promoted up and up until they're show runners, but they understand the production from a writer's point of view, and they have a writer's sensibility. And I have to say, from an actor's point of view, they're the best-organized shows I've ever done.

Now, forgive us, but we've got a plane at 4:30. But I did want to give you a chance to talk to my favorite screenwriter.

# SERMON AT SAGE CHAPEL

## JOHN CLEESE

APRIL 22, 2001

I AM TICKLED PINK that you have invited me to speak to you this morning. Thank you.

It must have seemed some kind of risk to request a sermon from a man once so widely accused of blasphemy. When Monty Python's *Life of Brian* was released in 1979, it was denounced by the Roman Catholic Archdiocese of New York as "blasphemous," by the Rabbinical Alliance of America as "sacrilege and blasphemy," and by assorted Lutherans, Calvinists, and Episcopalians as "profane." Indeed, the Roman Catholic Office for Film and Broadcasting actually made it a sin to see the film.

Surprisingly, because the Pythons, who could seldom agree on anything, were, for once, unanimous, in believing that *Life of Brian* was not an attack against religion. Our intention was to make fun of some of the ways some people practice what they claim is religion.

For Christianity, like the other great sacred traditions, can be received, understood, and practiced at many different levels. In addition, no matter what the founder of a sacred tradition may teach, there will always be people who understand the words quite differently. Taking literally what is meant metaphorically allows plenty of room for distortion, and people operating at a lower level of mental health cannot ever truly understand the teaching offered at a higher level. I always recall an advertisement in *Los Angeles* magazine in 1986 for Zen Buddhist Master Rama which proudly announced: "Buddhism gives you the competitive edge."

As was once said, "An idea is not responsible for the people who hold it."

Let us imagine, for example, that a small group of psychopaths decide to espouse Christian beliefs and create an organization called "Psychopaths for Christ." We can be sure that their interpretation of Christ's teaching would not be immediately recognized by, say, St. Francis. For one can be pretty sure that these latest converts would certainly behave in a way more psychopathic than Christian, although their behavior might not be better than if they had never been influenced by Christianity in the first place.

Now, if my use of the word *psychopath* seems extreme, let us not forget what has been done in the name of religion. Christians know about the Inquisition, the Thirty Years' War, and the Fourth Crusade to the Holy Land, which finished up attacking Constantinople, the seat of Eastern Christianity, as it seemed more profitable than fighting Muslims. Jewish people will know, for example, of Baruch Goldstein, who entered a mosque in Hebron during prayer in 1994, shot twenty-nine Arabs dead, and wounded seventy others. His grave has become a shrine, visited by scores of sympathizers. His tombstone reads: "Here lies the saint . . . Dr. Baruch Kapal Goldstein . . . blessed be this righteous and holy man . . . killed as a martyr of God."

And Muslims will know that, in the name of Islam, the Buddhists were eliminated from India in the thirteenth century, while today the Taliban routinely treats women as inferior beings and shells Buddhist sculptures. In Zanzibar, Dubash Meghji has religiously eaten one page of the Koran each day for thirty years. Although, in all fairness, we should note that Iran's Ministry of Interior has ordered people to stop stabbing themselves in the head during Muslim Shiite mourning rituals.

Ayatollah Ali Khamenei said: "Wounding one's head with daggers is not in the Islamic tradition."

Despite this clarification, it does seem that holy behavior can be very widely defined. But is it blasphemous to discuss these matters? I sincerely hope not. Because I am very interested in what the Dalai Lama had in mind when he spoke recently about "having a healthy relationship with one's religion."

The first relationship I had with a religion was with the Church of England 1950s variety, sometimes described as the Conservative Party at prayer. Eric Idle, who had a similar experience, wrote a piece in which a student read out his essay to the divinity class: "God created the world. And there is evil in the world. But since God is both omniscient and omnipotent, how could God, who is all good, have created evil?" To which the teacher responded, "Get out!"

I'll be blunt. Church of England religion, vintage 1950s, turned me away from religion for twenty years because I thought that's what religion was—great for some people, but not for me, and not for 90 percent of my friends.

However, in my mid-thirties, I found myself reading the odd piece about something called "Eastern Religion." I remember puzzling over *The Way of Liberation*, by Alan Watts.

The Ten Commandments must be obeyed because God is boss. But the discipline of yoga in Hinduism, or in the various forms of Buddhist meditation, do not require you to believe anything, and they contain no commandments. They do indeed have precepts, but they are really vows that you undertake on your own responsibility, not as an obedience to someone.

They are experimental techniques for changing consciousness, and the thing that they are mainly concerned with is helping human beings to get rid of the hallucination that each one of us is a skin-encapsulated ego—a little man inside our head between the ears and behind the eyes who is the source of conscious attention and voluntary behavior.

This appealed to something in me, but I was unable to square it with anything which I previously thought of as religion.

Then, partly as a result of being in therapy during the breakup of my first marriage, I read another Alan Watts book, *Psychotherapy East and West*, in which I read, "Psychotherapy is about analyzing the contents of consciousness; the sacred traditions are about taking an attitude . . . to the contents of consciousness." I somehow knew this was very important. But, again, I couldn't begin to connect it with anything that I had come across in church.

And then I had the huge luck—thanks be to God!—to read an essay delivered at UC Santa Barbara in 1959 by Aldous Huxley.

> There are two main kinds of religion. There is the religion of imme-diate experience—the religion, in the words of Genesis, of hearing the voice of God walking in the garden in the cool of the day, the religion of direct acquaintance with the divine in the world. And then there is the religion of symbols, the religion of the imposition of order and meaning upon the world through verbal or non-verbal symbols and their manipulation, the religion of knowledge about the divine rather than direct acquaintance with it.

He goes on:

> Let us begin with religion as the manipulation of symbols to impose order and meaning upon the flux of experience. In practice, we find that there are two types of symbol-manipulating religions: the reli-gion of myth and the religion of creed and theology.

Huxley then discusses myth, saying:

> It is unpretentious in the sense that it doesn't claim to be strictly true. It is merely expressive of our feelings about experience. But, although it is non-logical philosophy, it is often very profound—the most profound kind of symbolism.

He then points out that mythical religions are very frequently associated with what have been called spiritual exercises, but which are, in fact, psychophysical exercises. By their use, he says:

> The physical tensions which are built up by our anxious and ego-centered lives are released. This release through physical gestures constitutes what the Quakers called an "opening," through which the profounder forces of life without and within us can flow more freely. The Quakers were called "Quakers" for the simple reason that they quaked. The meetings of the early Quakers very frequently ended with the greater part of the assembly indulging in the strangest kind of violent bodily movements which were profoundly releasing and which permitted, so to speak, the influx of the spirit.

So, having mentioned the kind of religion that is more interested in experience, Huxley then talks about the religion of creed and theology, noting that it gives birth both to humility and the "proud prelate," both to St. Francis and Torquemada. He says:

> Religion as a theological system has always been ambivalent because of the strange nature of belief itself and because of the strange capacity of man when he embarks on his philosophical speculation and comes up with extremely strange and fantastic answers.

One thinks of angels dancing on the head of a pin. Huxley continues:

> Where you have theological systems, it is claimed that propositions about events in the past and events in the future and the structure of the universe are absolutely true; consequently, reluctance to accept them is regarded as a rebellion against God, worthy of the most undying punishment.

He sums up:

> The two types of religion—the religion of direct acquaintance with
> the divine and the religion of a system of beliefs—have co-existed
> in the West, but the mystics have always formed a minority in the
> midst of the official symbol-manipulating religions, and the rela-
> tionship has been a rather uneasy symbiosis. The members of the
> official religion have tended to look upon the mystics as difficult,
> troublemaking people. On their sides, the mystics have spoken not
> exactly with contempt—they don't feel contempt—but with sad-
> ness and compassion about those who are devoted to the symbolic
> religion because they feel that the pursuit and the manipulation of
> symbols is simply incapable in the nature of things of achieving
> what they regard as the highest end: the union with God.

Huxley concludes by saying:

> The religion of direct experience of the divine has been regarded as
> the privilege of a very few people. I personally don't think this is
> necessarily true at all. I think that practically everyone is capable
> of this immediate experience, provided he sets about it in the right
> way and is prepared to do what is necessary.

I read this seventeen years ago. And I am still puzzled why, in the
West, there's been so little interest in experiencing the divine and so
much emphasis on religion as crowd control. Is it because, once Christianity became the official religion of the Roman Empire, it attracted
as priests some who were unconsciously motivated by the desire for
power and who would therefore be both strongly motivated to seek
positions of power within the church and to add a power-seeking spin
to Christ's teaching when they were in a position to do so? As Vice
Pope Eric (*Monty Python* sketch) once said: "When you're propagat-
ing a creed of poverty, humility, and tolerance, you need a very rich,
powerful, authoritarian organization to do it."

Let me tell you about a cat, a truly wonderful one called Wensley. He and I have a special relationship based on affection and a strange kind of respect. But I have to tell you that smart though Wensley is, I am, forgive the boasting, a lot more intelligent than he is. I could say that my cat doesn't really understand me. For, if you asked Wensley what the purpose of life was, he'd probably say it was something to do with mice.

Now, here's my point. I bet that the gap in intelligence between God and me is rather bigger than the gap between me and Wensley. So, I find it hard to see the point of my trying to describe in words what God is like or what his or her purposes are because I might be foolish enough to believe that God might think just a little bit like me.

But, just as I can stroke Wensley and maybe make him feel loved and secure, I can conceive of the possibility that I might have an experience, a very slight kind of contact, a sort of divine pat, which might affect me at some deep level. People are changed not by exhortations to do things, but by experience. For example, people who have had near-death experiences or out-of-body experiences, whatever they may be, are changed by them in a way that could never in a lifetime be achieved by good advice.

And think what Christ asks us to do: "Love thine enemy." Can any of us begin to do this? It's a great aim, but how do we acquire the capacity? As far as I'm concerned, I might as well have been exhorted to move backwards in time. "Thou shalt hover unsupported four feet off the ground." Fine!

But now, I venture to suggest that egotistical little creatures like us could perhaps love our enemies and turn the other cheek—if we received some kind of divine experience. But under what circumstances might that happen? How would we improve the odds of receiving a divine pat? Which is why I'm so intrigued by Matthew 13:10–11: Jesus has just delivered the parable about the seed and how it falls on different types of ground and some absorb it and nurture it and others reject it. And, after that, the disciples come to him and ask, "Why do you speak to the people in parables?" And Jesus replies, "The knowledge of the secrets of the kingdom of Heaven has been given to you, but not to them. That is why I speak to them in parables." And he continues, "Thou seeing, they do not see. Thou hearing, they do not hear or understand, but blessed are your eyes because they see and your ears because they hear. For I tell you the truth, many prophets and righteous men long to see what you see, but do not see it, and to hear what you hear, but do not hear it." So there we have in the New Testament, in Matthew, a report that Christ is saying to his disciples, I'm giving you a teaching which I am not giving to the crowd when I talk to them in parables. And yet, all the teaching that has come down to us is the stuff given to the crowd in parables. We do not know what Jesus imparted to the disciples.

So, what could I do—what could we do—if we want to increase the chances that we might have an experience of the divine? Well, to start with, let me read you what Sogyal Rinpoche says in *The Tibetan Book of Living and Dying*:

> There are different species of laziness: Eastern and Western. The Eastern style is like the one practiced to perfection in India. It consists of hanging out all day in the sun doing nothing, avoiding any kind of work or useful activity, drinking cups of tea, listening to Hindu film music blaring on the radio, and gossiping with friends. Western laziness is quite different. It consists of cramming our lives with compulsive activity so that there is no time at all to confront the real issues.
>
> If we look into our lives, we will see clearly how many unimportant tasks, so-called "responsibilities" accumulate to fill them up. . . . We tell ourselves we want to spend time on the important things of life, but there never *is* any time.
>
> Even simply to get up in the morning, there is so much to do: open the window, make the bed, take a shower, brush your teeth, feed the dog or cat, do last night's washing up, discover you are out of sugar or coffee, go and buy them, make breakfast—the list is endless. Then, there are clothes to sort out, choose, iron, and fold up again.

And what about your hair or your makeup? Helpless, we watch our days fill up with telephone calls and petty projects with so many responsibilities—or shouldn't we call them "irresponsibilities"?

Our lives seem to live us, to possess their own bizarre momentum, to carry us away. In the end, we feel we have no choice or control over them.

It's clear to me that we're unlikely to have an experience of the divine while we're dashing around, ticking things off lists, caught up in quotidian details and pretty much unaware of our own existence. We're not going to have the sort of attention we need for a subtler experience while it's all being wasted on ordinary life.

So we need to be quiet. But if we manage to get quiet, what part of us might be able to get in contact with something on a different scale? Well, certainly not the more egotistical parts of ourselves. Surely they will be a barrier between the divine and the bit of us that could connect with the divine. That's why the poor (humble) in spirit are blessed, aren't they?

So, how do we begin to chip away at our egotistical shells to open up the more real, more simple, more childlike, more essential part of ourselves that God might be able to influence? The best stuff that I have ever read on this was written by a British psychiatrist, Maurice Nicoll, who studied with Georges Ivanovich Gurdjieff. He wrote:

You must try to struggle with your mechanical automatic behaviors, with wrong talking, with every kind of self-justifying, with all the different pictures of yourself, with your special forms of imagination, with mechanical disliking, with all varieties of your self-pity and self-esteem, with your jealousy, with your hatreds, with your vanity, your inner falseness, with your lying, with your self-conceit, with your attitudes, prejudices and so on. Expressly, you must struggle with your negative emotions, taken as a whole.

Sometimes you meet a person who is very eager and wishes to know exactly what to do. It is especially people who only have external attention and no internal attention who ask this.

As you know, our Work begins with internal attention. Self-observation is internal attention. A person must begin to see for himself what he is like and what goes on in him. For example, he must begin to see, through internal attention, his own negative emotions instead of only seeing other people's with his external attention.

He must see what it means to identify with his negative emotions and what it means not to identify with them. Once he sees this, he has got a key to the practical side of the work we must do.

The first stages are sometimes called "cleaning the machine." A person who constantly says, "What should I do?" after hearing the practical teaching over and over again is like a man who has a garden full of weeds and says eagerly, "What should I plant in it? What should I grow in it?" He must first clean the garden. So, we lay great emphasis on what not to do—that is, on what must be stopped, what must no longer be indulged in, what is to be prevented, what is no longer to be nourished, what must be cleaned away from the human machine. For none of us have nice new machines when we start our work but rusty, dirty machines that need a daily and indeed a life-long cleaning to begin with.

And one of the greatest forms of dirt is negative emotions and habitual indulgence in them. The greatest filth in a man is negative emotion.

A habitually negative person is a filthy person in this sense. A person who is always thinking unpleasant things about others, saying unpleasant things, disliking everyone, being jealous, always having some grievance or some form of self-pity, always feeling that he or she is not rightly treated and so on—such a person has a filthy mind in the most real and practical sense because all these things are forms of negative emotion and all negative emotions are dirt.

Now, the teaching says: you have a right not to be negative. It does not say: you have no right to be negative. If you will think of the difference, you will see how great it is.

To feel that you have a right *not* to be negative means that you are well on your way to real inner work on yourself in regard to negative states. To be able to feel this draws down force to help you. You stand upright, as it were, in yourself among all the mess of your negativeness and you feel and know that it is not necessary to lie down in that mess.

To say this phrase in the right way to yourself, to *feel* the meaning of the words, "I have a right not to be negative," is actually a form of mindfulness, of feeling a trace of your real identity that lifts you up above the level of your negative I's, which are all the time telling you without a pause that you have every right to be negative.

I have a real hunch that, if I could ever get quiet and free for a moment from my negativity, that I might get a gift from God.

Thank you.

# THE HUMAN FACE

**JOHN CLEESE** AND **STEPHEN J. CECI,**
Helen L. Carr Professor of Developmental Psychology

APRIL 28, 2001

JOHN CLEESE: I'll just explain why we are here. I've been interested in Steve's work because I met him almost the first time I came here, and we've always thought it would be nice to do something together. I've just finished a nightmare of a series for the BBC called *The Human Face*, which my secretary refers to as "The Human Farce." There are four programs in it and we're going to be talking about three of them today. The one we're not so much talking about is "Fame," which was quite interesting in its way but didn't contain much in the way of psychology or science. So this presentation tonight is about three of the programs.

The first program was kind of about identity. That is to say, the extent to which we are our faces and how much we are influenced by the way people look—we judge them on their appearances. The second program was about expressions: about how we make facial expressions, how we read them, how we fail to read them, and how we try to see people. That takes us into a section on lying which I think you'll find interesting. The third program was about beauty and it included an interview with a plastic surgeon in Los Angeles called Stephen Marquardt. His speciality was oral and maxillofacial surgery, reconstructing people's faces after accidents. He got fed up with not knowing what defined beauty. He happened to have training in mathematics, and what he has to say about the "golden proportion," if any of you have heard of that, is really extraordinary.

STEPHEN CECI: It's fascinating.

CLEESE: Yeah, we're going to come to that. But we'll start with a little bit to do with recognition. One of the things that I learned during the course of making this series is just to realize what an extraordinarily visual species we are.

I don't know if you know who David Attenborough is. He was on the program, and he pointed out that once we humans stood upright—you know, walking on all fours sniffing the ground, is a such a hassle—we became a very visual species. Once you stand up, you don't use your nose so much and then you start relying on facial recognition, which is why faces are so important.

CECI: And as you said in the show, which I thought was right on, was that we hang pictures of faces on the walls. We don't hang pictures of feet or hands. There's something about a face that we find intriguing.

CLEESE: Now, the interesting thing is, how do we recognize faces? The first TV program has got a lot in it about that. And we thought it would be fun to start off by showing you a bit from the program which talks about the fact that computer programs are being produced that recognize faces, and there's a particular one outside a famous football (soccer) ground in London. Let's have a look at that and see what we learn from it because, although it's lighthearted, there's a very interesting conclusion to be formed from it. What actually happens, as you will see, is that I tried to fool the machine. And I *did* succeed in fooling it.

CECI: Eventually.

CLEESE: Eventually, but with a disguise that you will be surprised the machine was fooled by.

*Video clip from* The Human Face:

JOHN CLEESE: *In East London, they are using state-of-the-art computer technology to clamp down on crime. They've stored images of the faces of hundreds of known criminals, and by scanning the streets with CCTV cameras, their face-recognition software can check faces in the crowd within seconds to see just who's out there.*

*To see just how good this machine is at recognizing faces, I've volunteered to put it to the test. The computer is interested in my vital statistics, nothing exciting, just measurements like the distance between my eyes are stored, as well as my basic mug shot. Once the camera homes in on my face, the computer measures it and searches the database for a match.*

SURVEILLANCE EXPERT: *The actual speed of the solution can be as fast as 15 million faces a minute; that's how many it can search through.*

CLEESE: *It's got me. But would it spot my cross-dressing?*

*It did not.*

*One last disguise . . .* [large dark glasses and a cap].

["INSUFFICIENT DATA" registers on-screen.]

*Bingo! I fooled the machine.*

SURVEILLANCE EXPERT: *John had a hat that was pulled down very low over his eyes and then made worse by these very, very dark glasses which had quite large frames, so we ended up almost losing that key area.*

*End of clip.*

CLEESE: Now, the point of that exercise is that disguise fooled the computer but it wouldn't have fooled a single one of you. You know, just pulling the cap down and putting on the dark glasses wouldn't have fooled you for a moment, which tells us the way we recognize faces is quite different from the ways these machines are trying to recognize one.

CECI: We trade off on the tremendous speed the machines have for feature recognition. We have, as humans, greater versatility and flexibility. Those kinds of mild disguises, as you just saw, throw off machines a lot more than humans. So do orientation changes. We have no difficulty at all if a loved one is shown to us in silhouette, or side profile, or three-quarter, or full-frontal. Machines find that much more difficult than we do. But it also reminds me that, while we can do these tremendous things, as you know, we're far from perfect ourselves.

CLEESE: Well, that's what we really want to talk about because Steve's done extraordinary work, as you probably know, on memory. It is really interesting when you start studying recognition because, on the whole, I think we're better at it than we think we are—or worse at it than we think we are.

CECI: Actually, it's both those things. We're better and worse. Sometimes we use these unconscious cues that we're not aware we have; we really have more memory than we know. But there are other times we think we can confidently identify someone and we're just dead wrong.

CLEESE: Well, I'm finding something, now I'm sixty-one. Somerset Maugham, the writer, said, "By the time you get to fifty, you've either met everyone or they look like someone you've met." I'm constantly finding with people that I'm not sure whether I recognize them or not. And it's like the phenomenon of memory. It's something we almost take for granted and then the more deeply we go into it, the more uncertain we become.

Steve's got a couple of good stories just to start with to tell us about this, and then we're going to give you some tests and this kind of thing. So, tell us about Odysseus.

CECI: Homer's Odysseus was the first documented case where someone, after being away for a long time—nineteen years—returns. His wife, Penelope, doesn't recognize him, the gardener doesn't recognize him. I think the only person who recognized him was an old nurse, and it was not because his face was familiar but because he had a scar on his leg that she identified. It really drives home how difficult it can be recognizing a face after there's been some aging or redistribution of fat.

And the first modern case we have like that, that I was telling John about earlier, is called the Claimant of Tichborne, and I find this a fascinating case even though we can never be sure who this fellow is. In 1828, a man named Roger Tichborne was born, and his family owned large holdings in the south of England and he was destined to become heir to those holdings. And after going through private schools and being tutored by a French tutor, he joined the army in the late 1840s and he served six years in the army.

And then, I think it was 1852, he was discharged from the army and he set sail from England to South America. This was 1852 to '53, he spent an entire year touring in South America, and toward the beginning of 1853, he set sail from Rio de Janeiro to Jamaica. But, unfortunately, there was a shipwreck and it was presumed all aboard the ship he was on, the *Bella*, perished. At least, that was the presumption. Now, we have a likeness of him that was preserved just before he got on the boat. It was taken in Santiago, Chile.

Presented on-screen: Sir Roger Tichborne, Santiago, Chile, 1852

That is the last definite likeness of Sir Roger Tichborne. As I said, it's late 1852.

So thirteen years pass, and on Christmas Day, 1866, someone shows up in England claiming to be the long-lost Sir Roger Tichborne, and here's a likeness.

Presented on-screen: individual claiming to be Sir Roger Tichborne ("the claimant")

He had been living in Wagga Wagga, Australia, for these thirteen years. He'd taken up the trade of being a butcher and had married a widow. He claimed that he had been rescued by an Australian vessel when his ship sunk and he had been living there until he heard rumors that he had inherited his family's holdings.

So when he arrived in England, five people made definite recognitions, including his mother. She is reported to have said, "It's my dear Roger. I'd recognize him anywhere."

CLEESE: And his sister.

CECI: Yes, his sister; but his brother, the solicitor, and his tutor all claimed he was an impostor—it was not Roger Tichborne.

So eventually there was a trial, a civil trial, to see if he was entitled to the holdings, and here's a picture of him just before the trial, and you notice he's put on considerable weight from the photo taken thirteen years earlier.

Presented on-screen: Tichborne claimant, England, circa 1871

You can see how much more slender his face was when he first arrived in England, and then as he got ready for trial and during trial, he literally doubled his body weight. You can see what that fat distribution does to the face. And this probably is why so many people were in such heated contest about whether this was really Roger Tichborne.

The court decided he was an impostor. The court said that he was a man named Arthur Orton, who was originally from Wapping, England, where he had been a butcher, that he then went to Australia and presumably found out an awful lot about the life of Sir Roger Tichborne. It didn't stop with the civil suit; there was a criminal suit following it and the claimant, now thought to be this person Arthur Orton, was found guilty. He was sentenced to fourteen years in a penal colony and, when he was released fourteen years later in 1884, this is what he looked like.

Presented on-screen: Tichborne claimant, a.k.a. Arthur Orton, England, 1884

He had lost a great deal of the weight. He looks a little bit more like the 1852 portrait of Roger Tichborne when he was in Santiago, Chile, than in the heavy pictures that intervened. But the two sides kept arguing about this. There was a man named Arthur Orton who was in an insane asylum in Australia and people said, "That's the real Arthur Orton. *This* is the real Roger Tichborne." And it was crazy because they had Arthur Orton's wife sail to Australia and she said, "Yes, that's my husband, Arthur Orton." They had a family member of Roger Tichborne sail to Australia and he said, "Yes, that's Roger Tichborne." So it was never really quite resolved to anyone's satisfaction. But it shows you just how difficult facial recognition can be.

CLEESE: Well, they're all sitting out there now feeling superior, aren't they?

CECI: Well, I think we should take them down a peg.

CLEESE: Yes, I think that's exactly what we should do.

CECI: Regress them to reality.

CLEESE: So, we've got a test for you guys.

CECI: Yeah, we have a test, and here's the test: A few years ago, my colleagues Patrick Cavanagh of Harvard, Maggie Bruck at Johns Hopkins, and I took advantage of a naturally occurring experiment. Patrick and Maggie had gone to the same high school and it was time for their twenty-fifth-year reunion, and many of the people they graduated with had not seen one another in the twenty-five years that transpired. So we wondered, would they be able to recognize the current faces of their classmates?

So we did the following: we took pictures of people today and we took their high school yearbook photograph from twenty-five years ago, and we scrambled the high school yearbook photographs. Let me just show you what it looks like here.

Presented on-screen: scrambled high school yearbook photographs, male

On the left are the high school yearbook photographs from twenty-five years ago, and on the right are these same people today scrambled with five new people. John thought that this would be lovely to drive you crazy. Can you match these people with their current visages?

CLEESE: Every one of the five on the left appears on the right, along with five red herrings.

CECI: So this fellow here [*points to the third photo down on the left*] was a high school photograph taken twenty-five years ago. Can you tell which of the ten men on the right is this fellow today? It's not very easy.

CLEESE: [*To a student in the audience*] Who do you think it is?

STUDENT: I think it's five.

CLEESE: Anyone else think it's five?

STUDENTS: Three, four.

CLEESE: There are a lot of votes for four, Steve. What's the answer?

CECI: The answer is five. But that actually is one of the easy ones. Here's one of the more difficult ones [*points to the fifth photo down on the left*].

STUDENTS: One. Two. Four. Five. [*Everyone laughs.*] Eight. Six.

CECI: We're all over the place. It's number four. John, whatever happened to those lovely hairstyles? Now let's look at some of the images of women.

Presented on-screen: scrambled high school yearbook photographs, female

CLEESE: Which one are we going to pick out for them to do?

CECI: Well, I'll give you a hard one and an easy one. This is a hard one in terms of statistically how many people got it wrong—number five on the left. Who is she today?

STUDENTS: Four. Three. Eight. Nine.

CECI: I'm hearing a lot of people say three, and they're wrong. No, it *is* three. This woman here is easier, number four on the left.

STUDENTS: Four. Two.

CECI: Maybe she's not easier.

STUDENTS: Six. One.

CECI: No, she's right here. Ten. Anyway, I don't think we need to belabor this, but it is kind of interesting how difficult this can be. It turns out that the better you knew the people in high school, the more classes you shared with them, the more time you spent socially (for example, dating), the more likely you were to accurately match them.

CLEESE: That's for a very surprising reason. It's not because you knew their face better, right?

CECI: That's right.

CLEESE: It's because you knew their personality better.

CECI: Exactly.

CLEESE: Which meant that you could better predict the sort of person they would become and how they would have their hair, right?

CECI: Exactly, all those things. It was a much more inferential, constructive kind of process, just as John was saying. Oh well, that's Bill, and I remember the kind of fella he was: today he would wear his hair a certain way, I would think, or he would or wouldn't have facial hair, or he would wear the following kind of clothing, and so on. It was really a much more inferential process. And, also, you weren't put off by changes in orientation so, you can see, some of these photographs from the yearbook are full-front, some are three-quarters, there are some side shots. And it doesn't matter—if you really knew the person well, it's just like picking a loved one out of a crowd. It doesn't matter if you're looking at a profile, three-quarter, one-quarter, or what have you.

CLEESE: And it seems to be putting on weight is the best way to avoid detection.

CECI: Exactly, more than losing hair or hair color changes, it's weight—it's the redistribution of fat. It seems to really affect the face, in particular.

CLEESE: I have a personal experience here. I discovered that the way, if I am going to disguise myself as an actor, the thing that people recognize most about me is this bit [*indicates his mouth*]. You wouldn't think that for a moment. And if I want to disguise my appearance, if I wear dental prosthetics, teeth that push my lips out like this, people actually don't recognize me. I don't know if you saw a rather unsuccessful film called *Frankenstein*. A number of my friends sat through that movie, not realizing I was in it. I did it because I didn't want anyone to smile as a reflex action when I first came up on the screen because Kenneth Branagh, who directed it, said: "If I get a laugh in this movie, I've failed." Usually, it's the other way around. So I thought it would be good to disguise myself.

In the program on identity, we investigated various ways we recognize people. Basically, we've got a storehouse in our brains, but we do not recognize faces feature by feature. It's a gestalt.

CECI: It pops out at you as a holistic gestalt. I'll say something about that in a little while, but nowhere is this problem of errors in recognizing faces more serious than in the criminal justice system, where, if you mistakenly identify the wrong face, the perpetrator stays at-large victimizing people, or some innocent person is incarcerated. The film clip you have is a perfect example of this.

CLEESE: Yes, in the program we show the clip, which we'll show now, and it is about a woman who recognized a man who raped her, and you'll get all the details here. It's a very, very interesting case.

*Video clip from* The Human Face:

JENNIFER THOMPSON: I had gone to bed early that evening and, around three thirty, was awakened by a sound.

Someone jumped on me and pinned my hands beside my head. I realized very quickly that it wasn't someone that I knew, and he proceeded to rape me.

First of all, I tried to adjust my eyes to whatever light was coming through my windows. Then, I just studied his face for scars, or tattoos, or jewelry, or facial hair. I probably had about fifteen to twenty minutes of total time that I looked at him, and I really tried hard to look at him, even though you don't want to, I did try very hard to keep focused and look at him.

CLEESE: Jennifer managed to escape from her attacker and describe him to the police.

CHIEF OF POLICE: I thought Jennifer was an outstanding witness for a number of reasons. She was able to articulate extremely well what happened to her during the course of the sexual assault. In addition to that, she was able to vividly provide a description of her assailant.

CLEESE: Jennifer went through the standard police procedure, describing her assailant, and then creating an identikit picture of him feature by feature.

THOMPSON: It was not easy. It's very difficult. I never really understood how many nostrils there are in the world, and how many lips, and eyebrows, and eyelashes, and bridges of your nose. There's just so much involved in a facial description. But once we were done, I felt fairly confident that the picture that we came up with was as close to the person who assaulted me as I could possibly get.

CHIEF OF POLICE: Within two days of the investigation, there were six individuals who had surfaced as suspects and we developed a photo lineup involving those six individuals.

CLEESE: Jennifer identified a young black man called Ronald Cotton as the man who'd raped her. Two days later, she was asked to come and look at a lineup at the local police station. Once again, she picked out Ronald Cotton. Even though she was severely traumatized, Jennifer was determined to testify at the trial.

THOMPSON: Well, I was very certain that was the person. Rage was filling up inside of me and, so, I think that I was very anxious to go ahead and proceed with the trial and see the man who attacked me serve his life sentence in jail.

CLEESE: At the trial in January 1985, Ronald Cotton was convicted of rape and sentenced to life. But Ronald had always protested his innocence and, once inside Central Prison in North Carolina, an extraordinary coincidence occurred which would change the course of his case. His cellmate, Bobby Poole, openly bragged to the other prisoners that he had raped Jennifer.

CHIEF OF POLICE: Bobby Poole did resemble the composite drawing, without question, but there are thousands of black males in this case who would, in fact, look like or resemble the composite drawing. So, that didn't force me to waiver [sic] my confidence of her identification.

CLEESE: In the appeal court, Jennifer was confronted with both Ronald and Bobby and, again, asked to identify the man who had raped her.

THOMPSON: When I saw both of them together, I remember looking at Bobby Poole and not recognizing him at all. I mean that, of course, one of the first questions is, "Do you recognize that man?" I said, "No. I've never seen him before in my life."

CLEESE: Jennifer's eyewitness testimony was so strong that Ronald was sent back to prison for another eight years. It wasn't until the new science of DNA testing was developed that her evidence was questioned. A long-forgotten sperm sample proved conclusively that Bobby Poole had indeed raped Jennifer. She had identified the wrong man.

JUDGE: It's the first time in a long time you're walking out of here a free man.

REPORTER: With these words, thirty-three-year-old Ronald Cotton was free for the first time in years.

THOMPSON: I don't think I ever felt so ashamed and guilt-ridden and, I guess, part of me was . . . I mean I felt like I had almost had . . . embarrassed, I think. Embarrassed that I had made such a huge mistake and that mistake had impacted Ronald Cotton for those eleven years. I mean, significantly impacted Ronald Cotton for those eleven years.

*End of clip.*

CLEESE: So, what I think is so interesting about all this is that, if these occasions ever arise in our own lives, we're much more likely to get it right or, at least, not get it wrong if we're more realistic about what our capacities to recognize people actually are. There seem to be general rules. First of all, lapse of time makes it difficult—particularly, accumulation of fat, body weight. But then, when you actually come down to recognizing people, in fact, when we know people very well, we're extremely good at recognizing them. Even, as you put it, from odd angles and in bad light. That's not a problem. We're actually very good at that. What we're not good at, at all, is recognizing people we've only seen once. And, of course, in most police lineups, that's exactly the case. Not only are we not good at recognizing people we've only seen once, but on top of that, there's all the emotional trauma.

CECI: That emotional trauma really degrades recognition accuracy. When you're under a great deal of stress, there's a long research tradition showing that you're not storing the images as well as you are when you are much more relaxed. And as Jennifer Thompson mentioned, the disadvantage of poor light, a strange person, and that she was processing the face of the rapist feature by feature, looking for scars, thickness of lips, and so on, and then, the photo kit also plays on that feature by feature.

CLEESE: Well, that's how it's been done in England for decades.

CECI: Here too.

CLEESE: And it's interesting, it doesn't work like that. That's not how we recognize people, so that's not a good way to achieve it.

CECI: You mentioned before that people who exhibit great accuracy in identifying faces seem to have this almost unconscious recognition that happens very quickly and very much a gestalt, very holistic, not feature by feature. A colleague of mine here at Cornell, Dave Dunning, who is a professor of psychology, has done research on this.

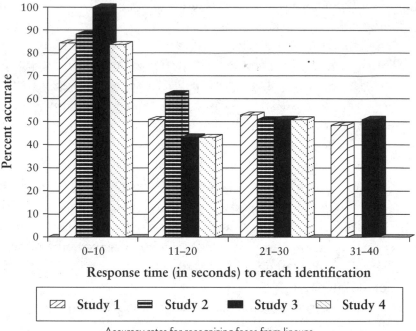

Accuracy rates for recognizing faces from lineups

This graph shows four different studies that Dave Dunning and his colleagues have done and the important thing is to notice these are accuracy rates, accuracy recognizing faces from lineups. Some people can pick the correct face out of a six-person lineup within ten seconds. Some people take longer than that. And in every study they've done, people who recognize faces quicker are far more accurate.

These are the reasons they give, those people who are accurate. They say things like, "I just recognized him. I can't explain why," or, "His face just popped out at me." It's that idea of the gestalt. If you look at the inaccurate people, they're more prone to say things like, "Well, the perpetrator had high cheekbones and number three has high cheekbones," or, "The defendant had a low brow and number four has a low brow." But that very particularistic feature-by-feature analysis, that's not how the human brain processes faces. It's done much more in this gestalt way.

CLEESE: The last time I was talking with Steve in the psychology department, I was actually doing a lecture called "Hare Brain, Tortoise Mind," about certain of the things we do almost effortlessly much better than when we try to think. And Steve told me about the ideograms.

CECI: Yes, there's this effect in cognitive psychology called a "sheer exposure" or a "mere exposure effect." So if, for example, we showed a lot of words on a screen tonight and then, a few days later, the people in this audience came in and we said that we had some anagrams for them to fill in, or to unscramble into words. Or we had word fragments, for example: "SC A BL D," "scrambled" with some missing letters. If "scrambled" was a word that they had seen when we were talking several days ago, they'd be much quicker at saying, "That's the word 'scrambled.'" Or if the letters were scrambled, they would be faster at unscrambling it than people who hadn't seen it. They're not conscious of having seen the word previously, because if you ask them, "Remember all the words that you saw?" they wouldn't remember that "scrambled" was one of the words we showed them.

CLEESE: I think it was ideograms. You asked the subjects to look at these Chinese ideograms which were flashed on a screen. The subjects were called in a week later and they were asked, "Can you recognize any of the ideograms?"

CECI: And they couldn't.

CLEESE: Not a single one. Then the experiment was set up a different way. The subjects were shown the ideograms and a week later they were shown them again. But instead of saying, "Do you recognize them?" instead, they were asked, "Are there any ideograms that you particularly like, that just appeal to you?"

CECI: "Are they pretty?"

CLEESE: Yes, "Are they pretty?"

CECI: And the ones that they *had* seen but weren't conscious of having seen they felt were prettier. There's an interesting moral there. When we have elections, especially in this country where you are inundated with the faces of the candidates, the first time you see, say, George Bush's face or someone's face.

[*Students groan.*]

I was actually thinking of George Bush Sr. You see, it's kind of craggy and asymmetric, but after you've seen it a hundred times, you start thinking it's prettier.

CLEESE: No!

CECI: It's true. Pretty much every public figure, people rate them as being more attractive after they've seen them a lot than they did the first time they saw them.

CLEESE: That's very interesting because this ties in to one of the things we explored in the *Human Face* program. One poor guy was having his face eaten away by cancer and a young woman who was absolutely delightful had this enormous lower jaw. She suffers from what is known as cherubism. And what I noticed was, and I'm being quite frank, when I first saw them, I kind of recoiled. Yes, there's a moment which—evolutionary biologists would say it's because it probably indicates a disease, so your initial reaction is to keep away. But after you get to know these people, you're simply not put off anymore.

CECI: I found when you sent me the videotape, the first time I saw it, I recoiled as well, and then I watched the video several times to take notes for tonight and the more I looked at her, the less I was shocked by her appearance.

CLEESE: That's right. You just get used to someone and then their appearance really doesn't matter. My wife and I know a famous sculptor who is singularly unattractive.

CECI: As a sculptor?

CLEESE: No, he's quite good as a sculptor. But now that we've known him for years, he's just him. You know what I mean? I used to think he was ugly. That's a bit encouraging.

To go back to recognition, there's one other point which was operating in this case of Ronald Cotton. And it is, and I don't mean this too lightheartedly, but it is the "they all look the same to me" syndrome. Because it is true that whites will recognize white faces better because we're better at differentiating them. You see what I mean. Japanese folk will recognize Japanese folk better because they're much more skilled at differentiating them. So if you're ever having to try and pick a face from a racial group you're not familiar with, you're much more likely to get it wrong.

CECI: One rule of thumb. If you ever are in a situation where it's important to remember across race, that one way you can foster transracial recognition is to do something that requires you to do more of a global gestalt process than a featural analysis. Such as, look at the face and make a judgment of how sympathetic the face is or how intelligent it is. As opposed to, do they have high cheekbones or what color of eyes, color of hair, or other featural aspects? If you do the more global process—is this a sympathetic or is this an intelligent face?—you're much more likely to recognize it later.

CLEESE: So that was a lot of the stuff that was in the episode on identity. The conclusion that I tried to get across at the end of the program is, let's try not to judge people on appearances—because we all do. It's an absolutely natural reaction, but it's one we need to hold back on because, if we get to know people better, we're probably going to have a very different impression of them, and there's also a slight problem because we do tend to hang on to first impressions. So, if we allow that first impression to be too strong, it could override some of the information coming in later and we may really get people wrong. What are we talking about next?

CECI: Well, we've talked about people being intrigued about faces for their attractiveness, for their intelligence, recognizing them in forensic settings. The thing we haven't talked about yet is being able to detect deception in a face.

CLEESE: That's right. One of the episodes is about facial expressions, and it's fascinating just to see how mobile the human face is. Somebody has figured out that we can make seven thousand expressions.

CECI: Is that right?

CLEESE: It's pretty astonishing. Apparently, there's one I'll try to do now [*blows out his cheeks*] which doesn't mean anything at all. But all the other 6,999 mean something, if we read them correctly. Of course, again, we are incredibly influenced by context. And something we didn't put in the program which might interest you—do you know the experiments that Eisenstein, the Russian film director, did? He did something which is very interesting. He just took a shot of an actor and put it at different points in movies. He used the same shot of the actor. And people—

STUDENT: Kuleshov.

CLEESE: Kuleshov? Are you sure?

STUDENT: Eisenstein too.

CLEESE: Kuleshov and also Eisenstein. They put exactly the same picture up, and depending on the context in the film, the audience looking at the face read in one face there was great compassion; in another, anger; and in another, mild amusement. So that just shows that reading expressions is actually incredibly tricky because, if we've got the context wrong, then it's going to work against our ability to actually figure out what the person is expressing. That interests me. That wasn't in the program.

CECI: That reminds me. Before we get into deception, I just thought of a very funny, but I think telling, example. A friend of mine in Canada, who is a cognitive psychologist, was at a conference some years ago—I'm thinking ten years ago. And he said to another friend of mine, he said, "Quick, hide me! My ex-wife is over there." It was this big exhibition hall where they had posters and people were presenting research on these posters. And she said, "Where?" And he said, "She's the one over at sector B, number 3, and I haven't seen her in eight years but I don't want to see her. And so, would you go up and find out what she's up to, what university she's at, and so on?" And it turns out it wasn't his wife.

CLEESE: Perfect. So what we're doing now is, having gone through this whole business of expressions, what we want to do now is to get to this business of lying. Okay? I think we should run the next excerpt. This is Paul Ekman, who is a terrific guy, now working with the Dalai Lama because he admires the Tibetan Buddhists so much and the way they control negative emotion and deal with it. He is the world expert on lying, so we got him on the show.

*Video clip from* The Human Face:

CLEESE: *Now, here's a little test. In this video are pictures either of happy chimpanzees frolicking in the jungle or rather bloody heart transplant operations.*

[*Live, referring to the program*] I'm asking the audience to guess whether I'm watching happy chimpanzees frolicking in the jungle or a nasty, bloody heart transplant operation.

*Oh, it's the chimps. Yeah, two of the little ones are fighting and there's a big one there. He's wondering whether there's food. One of them is getting quite cross.*

[*Live, referring to the program*] So, would you like to watch the film too? Let's have another look. [*Shows the heart transplant film.*] This is the basis, as you'll learn, of an experiment.

*Could you have told just by looking at my face that I was lying? In a similar test, Paul Ekman set out to find how good people were at spotting lies.*

PAUL EKMAN: *I took nursing students and what I did was to show them the worst scenes of medical gore that they might encounter. And while they watched that, they had to convince the interviewer they were talking to, who couldn't see what they were seeing, that they were watching a nature film. Now, I also had them see one of these nature films and describe it honestly.*
CLEESE: *Paul Ekman asked various people if they could pick the liars from this experiment. This is the moment when this young woman gives herself away. She's lying. But could they tell?*
     *And this is how nonexperts like us scored: no better than chance. Okay, so now we come to the experts, the people whose professions have given them*

*special experience with lying—police, judges, trial lawyers, forensic psychiatrists, and the experts who actually carry out lie detector tests. And here's how they scored: no better than chance. Judges, forensic psychiatrists: no better than chance. Police: no better than chance. The experts who carry out lie detector tests: no better than chance. Nobody could pick the liars. It's amazing. Except one group: a third of Secret Service agents scored 80 percent. What do they know that nobody else does? Using more recent footage, Ekman can show us what the Secret Service agents were spotting.*

EKMAN: *There is one sign of concealment, and that is a microexpression, an expression that's very reduced in time—about a twenty-fifth of a second is typical, while the normal facial expression is a half second to two-to-three seconds. In this experiment, we first found out what people had the strongest convictions about. The particular person I'm going to show you was asked his views about capital punishment. And then he was given the choice to either truthfully describe his opinion or to lie and claim to hold the exact opposite of his true opinion. So, let's take a look at him.*

MAN: *Personally, I think that they should be killed. I mean, should be executed.*

EKMAN: *Well, we've already seen a little microexpression in the forehead, and let me just back that up. Notice those little wrinkles, they're going to appear there, they're very fast. And realize what he's saying is, "Personally, I believe they should be executed." Okay? Now, if he's telling the truth and if he's confident about this, that probably shouldn't be occurring.*

MAN: *They should be killed.*

EKMAN: *That was a distressed expression: the corners going up, short wrinkles in the center of the forehead. We have the equipment to see these things. I can teach anyone in thirty minutes to see microexpressions which they didn't see before. When I teach policemen, it's the thing they like the most because thirty minutes later they could do some things they couldn't do before.*

BILL CLINTON *[video footage]: I want you to listen to me. I did not have sexual relations with that woman.*

*End of clip.*

CLEESE: I want Steve to tell us why he thinks the Secret Service agents were better at detecting a lie, because the fascinating thing is, the police were no better than any of us at telling whether people are lying because they think *everyone* is lying. And the reason they think everyone's lying is that anyone being questioned by a policeman tends to be anxious, and they send out anxious signals and the police make the unjustified jump of assuming they are anxious because they are lying. See what I mean? So a lot of things that we all think are signs that people are lying are only signs of anxiety, and there's no actual proof that the anxiety is directly allied with the fact they're lying. Does that make sense? So tell us why Secret Service agents were better?

CECI: I don't have a clue.

CLEESE: Does anyone else know?

CECI: Well, we've talked a little bit about it and your theory about this is as good as mine. My theory goes like this: the reason Paul Ekman's Secret Service are the only ones who score above chance—and it's only that subset of the Secret Service who actually conduct the investigations of threats against the president, *not* the people who ring the president when he goes outside. It's the investigators. The reason I think they're better than chance is because the consequences if they're wrong are enormous for their careers.

I don't know if any of you remember back in the '70s when Gerald Ford was president and Lynette "Squeaky" Fromme made a death threat against him. Does anyone remember that? Well, the agents went to her home and took her into custody, but let her go because she said, "Look, I wrote that death threat letter when I was drunk. I didn't really mean it." And they released her. And then several weeks later, as you know, she *did* try to shoot Gerald Ford, and I suspect that it wasn't very good for career paths of those Secret Service agents who let her go. So for that subset of Secret Service, experience results in direct, immediate, intense consequences if they get it wrong, and I think that's consistent with the other piece, which is what you feel about it.

CLEESE: Yes, I think that it's something to do with rudeness. I mean, I am British and, therefore, trying to be painfully polite all the time, and I find it difficult to stare at people because I know that it is rude and probably hostile. And I think to catch these microexpressions, I think you probably have to look at someone more intensely than you would normally under social conditions. And I think we don't like staring at people and making them uncomfortable, so we have to have a very, very good reason to do so. If you're in the Secret Service, I think you don't care a damn how rude you are because you're looking for someone who might be shooting the president. That overrides any questions of politeness and you are allowed to stare.

That's only a guess, but I'll tell you why I think that might be the case—because there's one other group of people they now know who are better than chance, and quite a lot better than chance, at knowing whether people are lying. I just want you to think for a moment. I will give $10 to anyone who guesses, not to someone who knows already.

STUDENTS: Mothers. Poker players. Used car salesmen. Customs agents. College students. Cancer patients.

CLEESE: Very close. People who have had strokes at least one year beforehand. Do you want to explain?

CECI: People with specific lesions in language areas of the brain, when they're looking at a face, they read whatever the face is saying, because their language processing is labored and segmental and a little bit behind. But they're really processing the face very intensely and it's not being interfered with by the verbal processing. So they're looking at the face and they're more likely to see microexpressions of deception.

CLEESE: I wonder if there's any evidence that psychiatrists—not police psychiatrists, psychiatrists in general—are any better at spotting lies.

CECI: We have a little bit of evidence that with children they're pretty poor. I can show you some of that.

CLEESE: Yes.

CECI: In our studies, we have children telling stories under one of three conditions. In one condition, they're recollecting something that really, truly happened. In another condition, they're out-and-out lying about it on purpose. In the third condition, they're giving a report that's completely false but they *believe* it, so we call it a false belief. And when child psychiatrists and psychologists are shown that latter group, they're not very good at recognizing the truth. In fact, if we could roll a piece of film from our lab—this isn't a very professional video, John, but it will drive home the message. Here's a little girl giving a report of something at her nursery school.

*Video clip:*

INTERVIEWER: *Do you remember what happened with Sam Stone at your school?*
GIRL: *Yes.*
INTERVIEWER: *You do? Well, I wasn't here that day and I want to know everything that happened that day when Sam Stone came to visit. Can you tell me what happened in your own words?*
GIRL: *My teacher said be careful with the dollies. Then he put it up. Then the dollies, some of them broked off.*
INTERVIEWER: *Some of them broke. The dollies were ripped up when he did that. Really? Well, why did that happen?*
GIRL: *Because he was throwing it up and down and he was trying to catch it.*
INTERVIEWER: *Oh, really. Well, was he alone or was he with somebody else when he did that?*
GIRL: *Alone.*
INTERVIEWER: *Oh, he was. Was he being silly or did he do that on purpose?*
GIRL: *He was being silly.*
INTERVIEWER: *He was? Well, did he do anything else?*
GIRL: *Then he got a book and throwed it up and the pages ripped off.*
INTERVIEWER: *Really?*
GIRL: *Then he threw one of the toys in housekeeping.*
INTERVIEWER: *In housekeeping? Up in the air, is that right?*
GIRL: *No, no, no. He did it in the hallway.*
INTERVIEWER: *In the hallway. Oh, not in the classroom? In the hallway. Oh, I see. Can you think of anything else?*
GIRL: *And then my teacher said: "Don't you throw another dolly." And he didn't.*
INTERVIEWER: *And then he was careful when she said that. Well, did he say anything to her?*

GIRL: No.

INTERVIEWER: Well, when your teacher saw that he was throwing things in the air, what did she say?

GIRL: That you need to go.

INTERVIEWER: You need to go?

GIRL: Yeah because you keep on ripping our stuff.

INTERVIEWER: Oh, did you hear her say that?

GIRL: Yes.

INTERVIEWER: You did. You heard her say that. Well, did you see him do that? Did you see him throwing things up in the air?

GIRL: Yes.

INTERVIEWER: You did.

GIRL: And I saw him ripping up stuff.

INTERVIEWER: You saw him ripping stuff. Do you remember a bear the day Sam Stone came?

GIRL: Yeah, he spilled some chocolate ice cream on it.

INTERVIEWER: He did? Did you see him do that?

GIRL: Uh-huh.

*End of clip.*

CECI: You can roll this little girl too. It's only about twenty-five, thirty seconds.

*Video clip:*

INTERVIEWER: Can you tell me what happened in your own words?

GIRL: Yeah. He looked around.

INTERVIEWER: He did? He looked around and then what happened?

GIRL: And then he went back out.

INTERVIEWER: Oh, then he went back out. Did Sam Stone do anything when he was there?

GIRL: [Shakes head no.]

INTERVIEWER: He didn't.

GIRL: *He just said hi.*

INTERVIEWER: *He just said hi. Oh, I heard something about a bear. Do you know*
*anything about a bear? A teddy bear.*

GIRL: [Shakes head no.]

INTERVIEWER: *Did anything happen that day with a teddy bear?*

GIRL: [Shakes head no.]

INTERVIEWER: *What about a book?*

GIRL: [Shakes head no.]

INTERVIEWER: *Okay. So, did you see Sam Stone do anything?*

GIRL: [Shakes head no.]

*End of clip.*

CLEESE: Steve, I want you to tell the audience, when the psychiatrists
watched that, what conclusion they came to.

CECI: We showed videos of these children to thousands of professionals, including well over a thousand psychiatrists and psychologists.
In fact, I have a slide here.

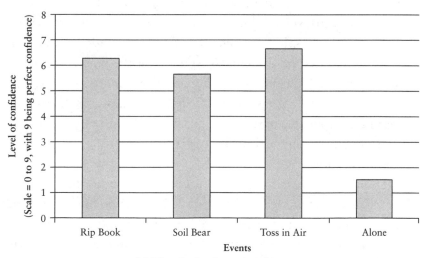

2,300 professional raters' confidence

We asked them, after looking at these videos, John, to tell us how confident they were based on what the children said. For example, do they think the guy ripped a book? And you can see here that the professionals are very confident that he ripped at least a page in the book. They're very confident that he spilled chocolate ice cream on a teddy bear, that he tossed something in the air. They're not sure about whether he was alone or with someone else. But the point is that *none* of these things happened. These were planted suggestions that the children had come to believe and, when the psychiatrists looked at that—I remember we presented these once to the annual meeting of the American Child and Adolescent Psychiatry Association, and there were, I think, 750 psychiatrists in the audience, and we had given them all these rating forms. And they got to that second little girl with the strawberry-colored hair.

CLEESE: Who was saying exactly what *had* happened.

CECI: Exactly. She was exactly right. She said, "He didn't do anything. He came in, he said hi, he walked around the housekeeping section, and then he left and said goodbye." And that's really all that he did. He didn't throw anything in the air, he didn't rip anything, he didn't spill ice cream on anything. But the psychiatrists—it was amazing, I still remember this—they argued with me. I said, "That second little girl, you all think she was lying." And they said, "She's in denial." And I said, "No, no." I said this out loud: "She's not in denial. You guys are in denial." And it's for the reason you mentioned: they're focusing on invalid cues. They were saying things like, "She's avoiding eye contact. She's twitching. She's nervous because she isn't able to tell you what she really knows." And I said, "No, she's just a shy little girl." But there you have it.

CLEESE: Question?

STUDENT: How were the children led to believe the story?

CECI: Oh, that sort of takes us beyond what we can do tonight, but we have a whole basket of methods to plant false memories in children.

CLEESE: The first time I met Steve, he told me about the kids reporting on the ambulance ride. Do a quick description of that one.

CECI: Yeah, that's just one of many techniques we use, but we can get children to create visions, to visualize or imagine things that didn't occur. So, for example, we say to children, "Do you remember the time you got your finger caught in a mousetrap and you had to go to the hospital to get it off?" And the first time you do that, they generate an image and it doesn't match anything stored in their memory, and they say, "No, I don't remember that. I've never been to a hospital. We don't have a mousetrap in our house." So we say, "Fair enough." And we bring them back the following week and we say, "Let's think about that again." And what happens is, every time you ask them to do this, they generate the image quicker and it's more perceptually detailed, so they start around the fourth or fifth week saying things like, "Yeah, I remember something familiar about the mousetrap on my finger and going to the hospital. I remember my mom and dad and brother put me in the van, took me to the hospital, and they put a bandage on it." And they give this very embellished, coherent narrative, with a beginning, middle, and end.

CLEESE: The boy's account is impressive because it's got so much detail in it.

CECI: Exactly. That's just one of the many techniques, but it's surprising how people can really forget what they know and think they know what they've forgotten. John, you've probably forgotten I loaned you $50 yesterday!

CLEESE: We have a film director friend called Michael Winner in England, a director of outstandingly bad movies. He's very, very funny and a great raconteur. He started to write his autobiography, and he recalled that the first time that he'd ever been excited by the prospect of film, he had gone up to a particular studio off the A1 motorway to see a series. There was an English series called *Meet the Huggetts*, and he went onto the set there and he met this young starlet called Violet Pretty. He'd been telling this story for years. So then, when he actually came to write his autobiography, he thought he'd check it out, and he found that *The Huggetts* was indeed a series, but they'd never shot it in this particular studio and that Violet Pretty had never been in one of these films. Everything to do with this story that he'd been telling for years was completely false.

CECI: Another aspect of false memory is crypto-plagiarism, where people sort of usurp the stories of their friends and take them as their own. A judge told me once that she was at her college reunion with her suitemates and they were sitting around telling stories and reminiscing about the olden times. She told this story about something that happened while on a date, and she said that there was this look of incredulity among her suitemates and they said, "Joan, that didn't happen to you, that happened to her." It's a real phenomenon.

CLEESE: I can tell you the creepiest thing that ever happened to me in that way. My mentor at the BBC in my early days of radio said that there were two Australian girls coming to London; they were twins and, if he gave me some cash, would I take them out and take them to the theater with a group of two or three friends and then go on to dinner afterwards. And when they sat down to dinner, one of them was ordering and the waiter said, "Would you like spinach?" And she said, "No, I don't like spinach," and then she looked at her twin and said, "Oh, no. It's you that doesn't like spinach."

CECI: Weird.

CLEESE: Talking of children, my wife is a psychoanalytic psychotherapist. She points out that the hardest liars to spot are the psychopaths, for a very good reason. They actually believe their own lies so they're so unbelievably convincing. There was a guy in Canada who was questioned again, and again, and again, and the police always came away thinking, No, he's so convincing, he didn't do it. Plus, he was very good-looking—because if you're very good-looking, you're much less likely to be suspected of a crime.

CECI: Well, if you're good-looking, you get lots of breaks in life, and the next segment really gets into what does it mean to be good-looking.

CLEESE: Yes. So we're going to talk about something from the "Beauty" program, and I mentioned this guy who is an oral-maxillofacial surgeon. In other words, he doesn't just tuck skin or something, he really reconstructs people's faces and their jaws and all this kind of thing. And he tells a story about how he sometimes reconstructed someone's face and wasn't really sure afterwards whether it was that much better than it had been before. And then he began really looking into what constitutes beauty, and he found out first of all that Pythagoras had got into this and had talked about certain proportions that tended to reoccur in nature.

Now, the interesting thing is, there was a thing called the "golden mean," but the Greeks had a rotten numerical system. Being able to do math depends on having a good numerical system. That's why the Romans, for example, were absolutely terrible at arithmetic. You try multiplying VII by IX. So you've got to have the right kind of system. The Greeks figured out what this proportion was that pleased the human eye, but they had to do it by geometrical means. If they described a couple of arcs, they could find out exactly where the point was on the line that was this proportion, et cetera. But it wasn't until the thirteenth century when a mathematician called Fibonacci came out with a series of numbers, and from this Fibonacci series one can work out what this proportion actually is. It's extraordinary. It is 1:1.618. Can you believe that? It's insane. And it happens to work. And Stephen Marquardt has figured it all out, and that's what we want to show you now. This will blow your minds.

*Video clip from* The Human Face:

CLEESE: *Do something like measure the distance from the floor to your navel and then from your navel to your head. If you are well-proportioned, the ratio should be 1:1.618, and that ratio is seen all over the beautiful body.*

STEPHEN MARQUARDT: *People started noticing it, artists noticed it, the math behind a beautiful face for example. Not any face, but it had to be beautiful. If the face was beautiful, the width of the mouth was exactly 1.618 times the width of the nose. If the face wasn't beautiful, that wasn't the case. Dentists in their dental work noticed that the upper front tooth was 1.618 times as wide as*

the next tooth over, the lateral incisor. So the central incisor was 1.618 times
the width of the lateral incisor, the next tooth over.

CLEESE: Wonderful. Give me some more results.

MARQUARDT: Your fingers. Your fingers are each called phalanges and each bone
in the finger is called a phalanx, and the phalanx that's closest to your knuckle
here is 1.618 times the phalanx that's in the middle, and that's 1.618 times the
size of the one at the end of your fingernail. So that was kind of amazing, this
number would come up over and over again.

CLEESE: [*Live, referring to the program*] Now, this is a young woman
who was chosen because she's a working model, and the interesting thing is some people think she's very pretty and some don't.

MARQUARDT: This is what's called a "golden divider." It divides distances into
1:1.618, which is the golden ratio. And in a beautiful face, we'll see that ordinarily
the width of the mouth is 1.618 times the width of the nose. It does, exactly.
    Show me your teeth. Smile. The width of the upper front tooth is 1.618 times
the width of the tooth next to it, and the same on the other side. The width of
the upper front tooth is 1.618 times the tooth next to it. It's amazing how this
proportion is repeated over and over again in a beautiful face.
    And the same with Zara, if I do the width of her mouth to the width of her
face, the camera should be able to see that the width of the mouth is 1.618 the
distance from the mouth to the corner of the cheek.

CLEESE: And it is.

MARQUARDT: Anyway, this relationship holds up over and over again in the face,
and Zara is a great example. That's why she's so pretty.

CLEESE: So Zara's face fits the golden ratio, and the golden ratio, 1:1.618, seems to
apply to all of them. Now, this idea that math can explain a beautiful face, any
beautiful face, has been taken even further by Stephen Marquardt.

MARQUARDT: If I look at the nose, the nose is a triangle. From the side view, the
nose is a triangle again.

CLEESE: And in a beautiful face, the sides of the triangle are 1.618 times greater
than the base and, from a triangle, you can build a pentagon.

MARQUARDT: What's the most attractive configuration of the face? The most
attractive expression? Smiling. When I smile, you start to see the pentagon.

CLEESE: Yes, I do.

*Stephen Marquardt combined pentagons and triangles all with the 1:1.618 ratio and built a mask. He claims that the closer a face conforms to his mask, the more beautiful it is.*

MARQUARDT: *Start with Kate Moss. Kate looks totally different from the others, but if I put the mask on her, you see that it's very close, and the interesting thing about Kate is that her eyes are preternaturally wide, or unusually wide. Her eyebrows fit beautifully, her lips, her nose, her jawline. Very, very nice. Even the hairline fits exactly what it should be.*

CLEESE: *And it's not just women. The same mask can be put on men, and Tom Cruise fits it perfectly. In fact, Stephen claims it fits any human face, so long as it's beautiful.*

MARQUARDT: *Here's one of my favorite actors—a star of stage, screen, and television. Let me just see how he fits. A handsome guy.*

CLEESE: *Oh, it's Paul Newman.*

MARQUARDT: *No, wait a moment, it's not Paul Newman. It's John Cleese.*

CLEESE: *Do you have a mustache grid?*

[*Live, to audience*] To my surprise, it didn't fit my face at all! Though Stephen had a good excuse for me.

MARQUARDT: *Quite frankly, it's very masculine. You see, the eyes are always narrower in a man and your eyes are narrower than the grid. The lips are thinner. You can see your lips are thinner here. Your nose is narrow, just like the grid. Actually, your nose is a little shorter, which is good actually.*

*End of clip.*

CLEESE: That's it. In case you didn't hear, Stephen was pointing out that the only reason my face didn't match the mask is that I am extraordinarily masculine.

Where do we go from here?

CECI: Well, it's easy to be dismissive about something as convenient as a ratio like that, but we know that starting at seventy-two hours after birth, babies prefer to look at faces that have been rated as attractive over faces that have been rated as average or less attractive. It doesn't happen fifteen minutes after birth. It takes three days looking at faces that they form this sort of prototype of what a face should look like. But starting at seventy-two hours, scientists have shown that babies reliably prefer to look at faces that have been rated as attractive. The one caveat, though, is that they're not necessarily proportionate or symmetric faces.

CLEESE: Really?

CECI: Yeah, there are some faces scientists use that are perfectly symmetrical and perfectly proportioned that raters don't think are very attractive, and babies don't look at those faces very much. Whereas there are some asymmetric and disproportionate faces that people think are attractive and they're the ones babies dwell on.

CLEESE: Well, when we started the "Beauty" program, we dealt with a lot of factors that are normally brought up over beauty. And that was before we got to Steve Marquardt. For example, the first thing is, all faces that are regarded as beautiful are basically youthful and healthy. So for example, good skin is incredibly important, white eyes, white teeth, all those things that indicate vitality as well as youth, very important.

Then you get into symmetrical faces—and that's fascinating because there's a guy called John Manning at Liverpool University who's been doing measurements on things like people's ears, and he finds that the best athletes have more symmetrical ears. In other words, the face is a kind of advertising board for the body—that the better your face is, the more symmetrical your face is, the better body you're likely to have.

CECI: I think, prenatally, from the time of the earliest cell divisions and alignments, if there are no infectious diseases or no threats in the environment, you would have perfect symmetry and, I think, what he's referring to is that perfectly symmetrical ears and eyes and so on are markers for general health and vigor.

CLEESE: That's right. Almost all the beauty indicators seem to be at the beginning to do with sexual attractiveness and fertility and all those things, and asymmetries indicate disease. Evolutionary biologists would say: "Ew, I don't want to mate with that person, not likely to have healthy offspring, not likely to have so many of my genes going on." You know, Richard Dawkins and all that stuff.

CECI: Don't you think, though, as we get older, we start to inherit the face that we've experienced? I think people's perceptions of attractiveness change.

CLEESE: Stephen showed me some pictures and I said I actually prefer the less conventionally attractive woman's face to that of another woman. He said that our choice starts to be affected by our experience.

And I remember years ago, a woman saying to me—this is twenty-five years ago—"I think that if you have a good sexual relationship with someone, you are forever after imprinted with that kind of face and you are drawn to that kind of face." And I've got to say, that's been totally my experience. Don't stare at my wife, but I very much like women with long faces. Now, that's nothing to do with what Steve says. Steve says if you take most fourteen-, fifteen-, and sixteen-year-olds, they will go like a guided missile for this grid, and then, as people age and get more experience, then we get a much more quirky kind of preference for a particular type of face.

CECI: Interesting. That also explains why you told me once you thought that Jamie Lee Curtis was very attractive.

CLEESE: Yes.

CECI: To each their own.

CLEESE: It's that very, very long face and nothing else at all.

CECI: Should we take a few questions?

STUDENT: If a child is stolen at a young age, how do they make a composite of a child that ages?

CECI: IBM, some years ago, developed some projection software where the essentially heart-shaped face of a child develops in an orderly way until adolescence, when there are some stresses and pressures that change it. The software is able to actually project our faces within certain epochs; so, within childhood to adolescence, and then within early adulthood, and then within middle adulthood, and then within aging, but not across those epochs. I think they do a pretty good job. It's amazing that they can take a picture of us at one point, make the projection of what we'll look like, and then we sort of grow right into it. But this isn't what is being done on milk cartons.

STUDENT: I understand that, if you take a half a dozen or so faces of different people and you find an average of them, that most will find the averaged face more attractive than any of the individual ones.

CLEESE: Absolutely right. Sir Francis Galton, who was a polymath genius, decided back in the late 1800s that he wanted to figure out exactly what criminals would look like. So he got a lot of photographs of criminals and he superimposed them to get the essential criminal face so he could say: "That guy's a criminal." Well, the trouble was the more he superimposed them, the better-looking they got. That's exactly right.

There's some guy up at St. Andrews University—we visited him but didn't use it in the program—who has specialized in averaging faces. Using a composite of fifty faces, you end up with a quite attractive face, but one which is strangely lacking in character.

CECI: In the "Fame" episode—which we are not using—there was one fellow who was a Chippendale model; he looked almost the epitome of perfection, but I thought it was a vacuous face.

CLEESE: Well, maybe he was just averaged by somebody. I think that may be the explanation. But what was so odd about looking at these composite faces was this sense of lack of character. When they averaged some better-looking-than-average faces, it produced a slightly better-looking composite face. But the thing about averaging, of course, it immediately brings in symmetry, so your subconscious is immediately assuming, "This is a face that doesn't have any disease." So that's partly why it's interesting.

STUDENT: In the face-recognition software they were using to spot criminals on camera in England, was the distance between the eyes the only thing they were looking at?

CLEESE: Well, distance between eyes is very badly put. Obviously, they mean proportions and I think that the key proportion was this and this [indicates areas of the eyes and the forehead]. So by putting on the hat and the dark glasses, it totally screwed the system, which is ridiculous. In fact, I was rather surprised that the police were quite happy to have this broadcast on national TV.

CECI: I bet there was an upsurge on sales of caps and sunglasses.

STUDENT: So, obviously physical attractiveness is correlated with whether or not someone is attracted to someone else, but what about emotional attraction?

CLEESE: Well, believe it or not, I helped somebody write a book about the emotional side once, so I can summarize that very rapidly. The man that I wrote the book with, Robin Skynner, said, basically, that we are attracted to people who have a similar emotional history, and that this is something that we pick up at an incredibly deep level that we're absolutely unaware of. And when they train family therapists, the first thing that they do before they've had any time to get to know each other, or even know each other's names, the first exercise that they do is that they're asked to circulate in a room and to choose someone who either reminds them strongly of someone in their family or someone they would like to have had in their family. They pair off, and those pairs then go off and choose another pair, and then they sit down and discuss their emotional history. It is apparently astonishing how often you will find a similar emotional pattern: that they lost a parent at an early age or that they traveled a great deal, something like that. Robin said he was never quite convinced about it until he was observing this exercise as a teacher and noticed two people who looked a bit lost and then chose each other and then they went off—there's no talk, this is just on facial expression—and chose another pair, and it turned out all four of them were orphans. So we're picking up stuff from each other whether we realize it or not, similar to the people who said, "Oh, I like that ideogram." We're picking up an amazing amount of stuff at an unconscious level—if only we could access it, if only we could trust it.

STUDENT: Early on in the discussion you had said that familiarity in a face is a great determinant of sexual attractiveness. And later on you went on to talk about proportion and symmetry. Is there any research on which one is the stronger determinant?

CECI: I don't know. I do know, because I know the infant work, that you can have faces that are not symmetrical nor proportionate, but between those two factors, I don't know which is the more potent.

CLEESE: I don't know if I'm reading this right: I think it's not so much that we're more strongly attracted by the faces, but as a slightly unattractive face becomes more familiar, we're not put off by it so strongly anymore. So I think it's a slight difference in emphasis.

STUDENT: In your experiments with the children, what did you do at the end of the experiment in order to help them face that Sam Stone didn't rip up the doll?

CECI: Well, we had the parents sit down with us when we debriefed the kids, and we explained to them that this is just in your head because you thought about it a lot and it didn't happen. But the fascinating thing—I remember John Stossel from ABC's *20/20* came to our lab and filmed some of this—the parents were sitting there with us debriefing the child saying, "No, you never got your hand caught in a mousetrap." The kid had given us a very elaborate narrative about, he was down in the basement, and his father was getting wood for the fireplace, and he and his brother got in a fight, and there was a mousetrap down there that snapped on his finger. And the mom said to him, "Billy, we don't have a fireplace in our house." And he said, "It happened in our old house." And she said, "But you weren't alive when we lived in our old house." So to answer your question, we have a lot of techniques but they're not all successful.

STUDENT: Do attractive faces lose that beautiful proportion over time?

CLEESE: Yes, they do. Sometimes fatally so. The proportions of our face change when we get older.

CECI: As important as attractiveness is for getting better verdicts in court and being given the benefit of the doubt in society, when we show men in a computer-dating situation—"Here are all these photographs," say, of women who have applied, "Pick which one ideally you would like to go out with"—they don't pick the most attractive faces. They tend to pick the faces that are closer to themselves in attractiveness level.

CLEESE: Oh, really? We interview David Buss, who's one of the experts on long-term relationships, and David Buss says there are two types of relationships. There's the quick affair, the one-night stand, the sexual whatever. And then, when people start looking for a long-term relationship, they look for quite different things and it's quite surprising. In a funny way, and rather encouragingly, the two things that are much the most important are kindness and intelligence; that's in the long-term partner. It doesn't stop people's eye from roving sometimes, but that's what they're looking for when they're looking for a long-term relationship.

There's one other interesting thing I wanted to mention, and there's an argument about who said this—George Orwell, or Abraham Lincoln, or Mickey Mouse, or someone else said: "A man is responsible for his face after the age of forty." Or fifty, depending on whether it was Lincoln or Orwell. The reason is that, early on, you cannot tell from somebody's face whether they're nice or a complete shit. You absolutely can't tell. But as you get older, what happens is that people's expressions, their kind of permanent expression, if they're cheery, they're kind of cheery, if they're miserable, they're kind of miserable, if they're tight, they're tight. Those states start imprinting themselves onto people's faces and, by the time you get to forty, you can begin to see the laugh lines or the droop lines, the sort of meanness, or the habitual expression. Then, at that point, you can begin to see what sort of person is behind the face. You can begin to rely on the face, but not until that kind of age. And then another interesting thing—as people get much older, we find that we're very, very drawn to faces that seem to embody virtues or qualities that we admire. So you see somebody like the Dalai Lama, it's not necessarily a beautiful face but there's something about that face that touches us deeply.

CECI: Wisdom and such.

CLEESE: And, of course, that kind of beauty is earned, whereas the other kind of beauty is definitely unearned.

CECI: The moral is, buy your used cars from fifty-year-olds.

STUDENT: What about someone like Joan Rivers?

CLEESE: Well, she was actually in the program doing jokes. I think Joan is quite open about the fact that she's had a lot of plastic surgery. She raised the question, What do we think about plastic surgery? But Stephen Marquardt is very, very clear about this. For younger people who, for some reason, don't feel good about their looks, plastic surgery can transform their lives. But if you were born beautiful and plastic surgery is about hanging onto it, then you get into difficult areas because, if you are beautiful, Steve was saying that you get better jobs if you're good-looking, better jury verdicts—there are all these extraordinary advantages to being good-looking, which is known as the "halo effect." But, of course, if you are stunningly beautiful, you don't bother to develop your other qualities. This is a point that my wife made, and we managed to get it into the program. This is something that happens. People who rely on their looks don't develop other parts of themselves, and then when they get to forty and start losing their looks, they don't have anything else, so they're really terrified. And that's when they resort to plastic surgery.

We interviewed a marvelous photographer. He's photographed every beautiful woman in the world, and he said two really fascinating things. One was, "They all need a bit of help." It's very interesting. The other one was, "The trouble with plastic surgery is, if you look closely, some bits look old and some bits look new." But, of course, if you're in Los Angeles, it's genuinely different there because so many people have had plastic surgery that you begin to look slightly odd if you haven't had it. I'm being serious.

STUDENT: This is just a comment. I had a dream about you.

CLEESE: It's nothing unusual.

STUDENT: I saw you in a crowd of people and a lot of the people had very unpleasant and crusty looks. You were in the crowd and you had a very radiant, happy, and calm presence.

CLEESE: It's true. It's all true.

CECI: That was no dream.

STUDENT: It shows you have a very good life.

CLEESE: Either that, or I'm a very good actor.

# WHAT IS RELIGION? MUSINGS ON *LIFE OF BRIAN*

## JOHN CLEESE

FIRST-YEAR FAMILY WEEKEND
OCTOBER 22, 2004

**Introduction, Cornell President Jeffrey Lehman:** Good evening. We are thrilled to have John Cleese here at Cornell as an Andrew Dickson White Professor.

*Life of Brian* is Monty Python's 1979 satire of organized religion. It was recently rereleased and we showed it twice last month. The movie annoyed a lot of people when it was first released twenty-five years ago and it continues to generate controversy. It also provided inspiration for Professor Cleese's talk tonight.

**John Cleese:** I am nervous tonight because I hope you are not expecting a cabaret with musical numbers and banjo playing or anything like that. I have been asked to talk to you, probably because I am a celebrity, and I am happy to do that. My only problem will be stretching about twenty-two minutes' worth of material out to two and a half hours.

There's one other thing that makes me nervous. There may be some scholars here who know much more about what I am talking about than I do, which is the reversal of the ideal situation where the speaker should have some information that his audience does not already possess. Never mind. I am a celebrity. And that's all that matters these days . . . except that it's always good to be topical.

It is a bit topical that Monty Python's *Life of Brian* has just been rereleased. People are saying to me that the rerelease is just a cynical bit of marketing to try to get as much attention for the movie as possible in the wake of *The Passion of the Christ*. Which, of course, is true. It's our attempt to get our thirty pieces of silver on the back of tiny Mel Gibson and, if possible, to annoy him. Because, as Jeff said, *Life of Brian* did annoy many people when it first came out in 1979. There were large numbers of people protesting outside the cinemas. I remember a banner that said: "Monty Python is an agent of the devil." I remember thinking, "I'd love to be on 10 percent of what he makes." And there were denunciations. We were condemned by the Jewish Orthodox folk, the Jewish liberal folk, the Catholics, the Lutherans, and the Calvinists. And we were very proud about that because, as Eric Idle said, "We've given them the first thing they've agreed on for five hundred years." So I like to think of us Pythons as "uniters." I think that *Life of Brian* is our best film. I really do. And it always slightly surprises me that in America, people seem to prefer *The Holy Grail,* whereas in Britain everyone prefers the *Life of Brian*; I have to say I do agree with that.

But what was unusual about the film was that we were actually able to agree on the content, in the sense that we were able to agree on what religion *isn't*. We certainly could have never agreed on what it *was*, because we as a group could agree on very little, except the need for good food and wine. But in this particular case, there was serendipity about our views, which was very unusual. It all started because we'd just made *The Holy Grail*, which had been very successful. We were sitting in a restaurant in Soho in London and someone suggested that we do a comedy film based on the Gospels. So we all giggled a bit, and then Eric Idle said it should be called *Jesus Christ: Lust for Glory* because Jesus *did* become extraordinarily famous. I think one could say he was a celebrity.

We formed the idea that there was a thirteenth disciple called Brian, who was always being invited to the big events but he could never make them because he had a somewhat demanding wife. For example, he was invited to the Last Supper, but his wife had already invited friends around for dinner so Brian asked if he could come on afterwards for a drink; or he heard something about the Garden of Gethsemane and he thought it was the nightclub of that name. So, having decided that, we all sat down and wrote a completely different movie because it wouldn't have been very creative to stick to what we'd agreed! And this movie is, in fact, about someone who was born right next to Jesus Christ, literally in the next manger. And at a much later point in his life, Brian is not only chased by the Romans because he gets mixed up with a revolutionary group but he's also, quite mistakenly, recognized as a messiah by a group of people who are not particularly good at recognizing messiahs. And in this way, we were able to make jokes not about religion—I really ask you to take that point very seriously—*not* jokes about religion but about the way some people pursue religion.

So, I'd like to start with a brief extract, only two and a half minutes, that leads me into the first point I'd like to make. Brian and his mother turn up to hear the preaching of this person about whom they've heard, called Jesus Christ.

*Video clip from* Life of Brian:

JESUS CHRIST: *How blessed are those who know that he's of God. How blessed are the sorrowful; they shall find consolation. How blessed are those of gentle spirit; they shall have the earth for their possession. How blessed are those who hunger and thirst to see right prevail; they shall be satisfied. How blessed are those whose hearts are pure; they shall see God.*
MOTHER: *Speak up!*
BRIAN: *Sssh, quiet, Mum!*
MOTHER: *Well, I can't hear a thing. Let's go to the stoning!*
BIGNOSE: *Sssh!*
BRIAN: *You can go to a stoning any time.*
MOTHER: *Ah, come on, Brian!*
BIGNOSE: *Will you be quiet!*

*BIGNOSE'S WIFE: Don't pick your nose!*

*BIGNOSE: I wasn't picking my nose. I was scratching it.*

*BIGNOSE'S WIFE: You was picking it while you was talking to that lady!*

*BIGNOSE: I wasn't!*

*BIGNOSE'S WIFE: Leave it alone! Give it a rest!*

*WISEGUY: Do you mind? I can't hear a word he's saying.*

*BIGNOSE'S WIFE: Don't you "do you mind" me! I was talking to my husband!*

*WISEGUY: Well, can't you talk to him somewhere else? I can't hear a bloody thing!*

*BIGNOSE: Don't you swear at my wife!*

*WISEGUY: Well, I was only asking her to shut up so that I can hear what he's saying, Bignose!*

*BIGNOSE'S WIFE: Don't you call my husband "Bignose"!*

*WISEGUY: Well, he has got a big nose.*

*BEARDED MAN: Could you be quiet, please? What was that?*

*WISEGUY: I don't know; I was too busy talking to Bignose!*

*SPECTATOR #1: I think it was: "Blessed are the cheesemakers."*

*BEARDED MAN'S WIFE: Aha, what's so special about the cheesemakers?*

*BEARDED MAN: Well, obviously it's not meant to be taken literally; it refers to any manufacturers of dairy products.*

*End of clip.*

I like that scene because it's about how, first of all, we can always get distracted from anything, no matter how important it is. But it also raises the question of how much of what we read in the Bible is *really* what Jesus said. I mean, many scholars believe Mark is the earliest Gospel. I've been trying to find a date; some people are very confident and say it was written about 64 AD. Other people say it's quite a lot later, but it was probably written thirty to seventy years after Christ's death. There is a source prior to that, which Biblical scholars call "Q," short for Quelle, which is the German word for *source*, and they think that Quelle provided material for both Luke and Matthew. And that seems to have been written down somewhere between 20 and 70 AD—that's the best they know. But what's in Luke and Matthew is a different tradition from what you get from Saint Paul's letters to his various communities. So it immediately raises the all-important question of how much of what's in the New Testament is really what Christ was teaching.

And, in a sense, that's what's always interested me. For example, if you take the very critical bits in the New Testament about the Jews, well, all the early Christians were Jews so what's *that* all about? Clearly, all the good guys are Jews and all the bad guys are Jews. Everybody's Jews. So you can hardly claim that it's particularly one side or the other. If you think that around 60–70 AD, the Christians were being badly persecuted in Rome by Emperor Nero, and that around the same time there was a great revolt in Judea against the Roman occupying forces, which wasn't put down for four years. And if you think that during this period, the Romans do not like the Jews because they're the most troublesome, difficult group to govern in the entire Roman Empire—the ones who are most resistant to the idea of the Pax Romana, the peace imposed on the world by the Romans. So would it be surprising if these critical remarks about the Jews were put in so that the Christians in Rome, let's say, were able to distance themselves from these troublesome people? And would it not help the Romans to feel more kindly disposed towards the Christians if there were one or two positive references to Romans, like the centurion who's standing under the cross and says, "This surely is the son of God"? Or the Roman centurion who was given as an example by Jesus as someone who could really understand what Jesus meant by the word "faith": "I tell you, not even in Israel have I found such faith."

So, it seems to me, it would have been perfectly understandable and excusable for persecuted Christians to add this kind of stuff into the documents that already existed to try and reduce the extent of the persecution, to try and make themselves more sympathetic to the Romans. I've always been fascinated by the gap, which sometimes seems to me enormous, between the normal dogma of the organized Christian churches and what Christ himself actually taught.

I once wrote a mean-spirited and ignorant and poorly researched piece, which I'd like to read to you. I was lucky enough to get an interview with Vice Pope Eric and I asked him, "What is the Catholic position on sex?" And he said, "Well, our main worry at this point is intramarital sex." And I said, "Sex within the marriage?" And he said, "Well, you see, it is within marriage that most people tend to forget that most of this carnal knowing actually takes place." And I said, "But that isn't wrong, from a Catholic point of view?" And he said, "Actually, it is. I mean, we don't often come right with it, because our problem is, like it or not, sex is, at the moment, still the best way we've got of reproducing ourselves. But we certainly recommend virgin births whenever possible. They are certainly preferable. But we can't rely on them at this point, so for purely practical reasons we've been forced to turn a blind eye to intramarital sex, but only, of course, for outnumbering purposes, certainly not for fun." And I said, "Vice Pope, did Christ himself say anything about sex being sinful?" And the Vice Pope said, "Apparently not. No, this was an oversight on his part which, fortunately, we've been able to correct with some help from the teachings of Paul." And I asked, "Does this necessity to re-edit Christ sometimes worry you?" And the Vice Pope says, "Well, not really. After all, you cannot treat the New Testament as gospel; one must remember that Christ, though he was a fine young man with some damn good ideas, did go off the rails now and again. You know, rich man, eye of needle, that sort of thing." And I said, "With certain exceptions, you do accept his teaching?" And the Vice Pope said, "It's been an invaluable basis for our whole operation, really. Of course, people sometimes accuse us of not practicing what he preaches, but you must remember that, if you are trying to propagate a creed of poverty, gentleness, and tolerance, then you need a very rich, powerful, authoritarian organization to do it."

Now, if I were more of a scholar, I would be able to take you properly through the gaps between Christ's teachings and those of organized Christianity. For example, I attended a Church of England school from the age of eight to eighteen, and there was a Protestant service every single day of that schoolboy life of mine, so I heard a lot of Bible readings. I do not remember Christ ever claiming that his mother was a virgin, and I don't remember his talking about hell.

Father Thomas Keating, the Benedictine monk, points out that when the very, very rich young man comes to Jesus and says, "What must I do?" Jesus says, "Well, you must sell it all, give it away, give it to the poor, then you can follow me." The young man doesn't want to do that, so he goes away. And Jesus lets him go; he does not threaten him with hell.

In addition, if you think how Jesus is usually portrayed, as this tremendously sad, pain-wracked figure hanging from a cross, well, there's no question at all, I'm afraid—*that* is a graven image which, of course, is specifically forbidden by the Ten Commandments. And usury, which meant lending money for interest, was a sin for the first fifteen hundred years of the Christian era as far as the church was concerned; they kind of revised that when capitalism got going. So it goes to show that what is put forward as Christian dogma is, at the very least, pragmatic.

There's a marvelous book about this strange problem by Jacob Needleman, called *Lost Christianity*. And you see, the reason I think it's so important is that if you think of Christ's teaching, you know, Christ says, "Love your enemy." That is simply beyond my emotional capacity. And it strikes me that possibly there is some missing teaching that would enable me to develop psychologically or spiritually to the point where I could eventually reach this very advanced stage of spiritual development—where I *could* love my enemy. But the instructions seem to have gone missing. We see in Mark 4:33–34:

With many similar parables, Jesus spoke the Word to them, as much as they could understand. He did not say anything to them without using a parable.

But when he was alone with his own disciples, he explained everything.

Could the conditions for an experience of the divine have been part of the esoteric instructions that Christ gave his disciples?

Christ clearly was a mystic. I mean, there's not the slightest doubt about that. And the question I would ask is, why did I—growing up ten years in the Church of England—why did I hear so little of mysticism, given that Christ was a mystic? I mean, I never considered this puzzle properly until I found a series of lectures given by Aldous Huxley in 1959 in Santa Barbara. According to Huxley, there are two types of religion. One is mystical, seeking a personal experience of, or communion with, God. The other is more of a social organization, manipulating and interpreting symbols and words, and it is this institutional religion that has been the most important in the West.

The organized religions have always been rather uneasy about mystics. They have tended to look down on them as unruly people dashing off and having mystical experiences without getting permission. On their side, the mystics are not really interested in nonspiritual matters, the institutional and administrative side of the organized church. For them, the highest aim is union with the divine.

Now, in the Protestant Christianity that I grew up with, nothing was ever mentioned about this kind of thing. It was all about religion as crowd control: you must believe this, you have to do that, *or else.* It's crowd control.

So, here's an excerpt from *Life of Brian.* It's about stoning someone who is blaspheming against Jehovah by saying Jehovah's name out loud.

*Video clip from* Life of Brian:

CROWD OF WOMEN: [Yelling.]
JEWISH OFFICIAL: *Matthias, the first son of Deuteronomy of Gath.*
MATTHIAS: *Do I say, "Yes?"*
STONE HELPER #1: *Yes.*
MATTHIAS: *Yes.*
OFFICIAL: *You have been found guilty by the elders of the town of uttering the name of our Lord, and so, as a blasphemer, . . .*

CROWD: Ooooh!

OFFICIAL: . . . you are to be stoned to death.

CROWD: Ahh!

MATTHIAS: Look. I—I'd had a lovely supper, and all I said to my wife was, "That piece of halibut was good enough for Jehovah."

CROWD: Oooooh!

OFFICIAL: Blasphemy! He's said it again!

CROWD: Yes! Yes, he did! He did!

OFFICIAL: Did you hear him?!

CROWD: Yes! Yes, we did! We did!

WOMAN #1: Really!

[CROWD is silent.]

OFFICIAL: Are there any women here today?

CROWD: No. No. No. No. . .

OFFICIAL: Very well. By virtue of the authority vested in me—

[CULPRIT WOMAN stones MATTHIAS.]

MATTHIAS: Oww! Lay off! We haven't started yet!

OFFICIAL: Come on! Who threw that? Who threw that stone? Come on.

CROWD: She did! She did! He did! He! He. He. Him. Him. Him. Him. He did.

CULPRIT WOMAN: Sorry. I thought we'd started.

OFFICIAL: Go to the back.

CULPRIT WOMAN: Oh, dear.

OFFICIAL: Always one, isn't there? Now, where were we?

MATTHIAS: Look. I don't think it ought to be blasphemy, just saying "Jehovah."

CROWD: Oooh! He said it again! Oooh! . . .

OFFICIAL: You're only making it worse for yourself!

MATTHIAS: Making it worse?! How could it be worse?! Jehovah! Jehovah! Jehovah!

CROWD: Oooooh! . . .

OFFICIAL: I'm warning you. If you say "Jehovah" once more—

[MRS. A. stones OFFICIAL.]

Right. Who threw that?

MATTHIAS: [Laughing.]

[Silence.]

OFFICIAL: Come on. Who threw that?

*CROWD: She did! It was her! He! He. Him. Him. Him. Him. Him. Him.*

*OFFICIAL: Was it you?*

*MRS. A.: Yes.*

*OFFICIAL: Right!*

*MRS. A.: Well, you did say "Jehovah."*

*CROWD: Ah! Ooooh! . . .*

[CROWD stones MRS. A.]

*OFFICIAL: Stop! Stop, will you?! Stop that! Stop it! Now, look! No one is to stone anyone until I blow this whistle! Do you understand?! Even, and I want to make this absolutely clear, even if they do say "Jehovah."*

*CROWD: Ooooooh! . . .*

[CROWD stones OFFICIAL.]

*WOMAN #1: Good shot!*

[Clap, clap, clap.]

*End of clip.*

Now, the interesting thing about that scene was, when the movie came out, the rabbis got very angry about it. It's interesting, isn't it? Why did they get angry? I mean, stonings happened. Perhaps people don't like being reminded of when they behaved badly and, of course, anger is much easier on the ego than shame. You get a similar reaction today to whistleblowers. Perhaps it's naïve to expect people to say, "Thank you for pointing this out to us; now we can do something about it." But it's a reasonable ideal. I have to say that the Catholics are better than the rabbis in this case because at least they pay hush money.

Now stoning, I think, is symbolic of the violence that's inherent in most organized religion. And, you know, Christianity does have an outstanding record in this respect. You know, wars, inquisitions, torturing people to death if necessary.

I was in San Gimignano in Tuscany about five years ago with my family, and we decided that we were going to see an exhibition of torture implements and instruments. They were mostly ones used by the church. There was one particular one that stuck in my mind because the instructions on how to use it were so precise. The person was strapped, with their arms above their head, and then five candles were placed on each side of them so that the flames burned that particular point of the body, and five were placed on this side. You can imagine what one was like and then multiply that by ten. But what was fascinating was that the length of the candle was exactly specified down to the last millimeter and the distance from the flesh, as though it was a matter of extreme administrative diligence so that no one would have a chance of getting their rocks off. And it was extraordinary to see how it was being sanitized.

And also, before anyone was tortured, the previous evening, if a confession was required, the church folk would take them down and show them the instruments of torture. You know, this is the stuff that we're going to heat until it's red hot and then we'll clamp it on your flesh, you see, and tear it off the bone, this kind of thing. So if you'd like to confess now, it's entirely up to you, and then we won't have to do that to you in the morning.

And that was the basis of a lot of the compulsion for people to believe what they were told was the message of Christ. There's also another extreme threat of violence if you think of the notion of hell. You know, people having red-hot tongs pressed against their flesh for eternity. I mean, you folk couldn't watch it for five seconds, bless you. And yet hell is a major part of Christian teaching.

And hell is not only for bad people, it's also for the unconverted. And I love what a retired professor of philosophy, called Raymond Smullyan, says about this. He says:

> The dilemma is this. If it is really true that the unconverted will suffer eternal punishment, then my deceased parents, my family, my best friends, all those I love dearly are scheduled for eternal torture. Now, if God wants this, if he is the cause of this, then I would, of course, fear God. But I would find it impossible to love him because he'd be my worst enemy. On the other hand, if God did his best to help my loved ones, but was unable to, then the cause of

their suffering would be outside God. In which case, I would love God for trying to help, but I would have no reason to fear him. Why would I fear a friend? What I would then fear is whatever it is, something outside God that was the cause of damnation.

And he goes on:

I think it's high time that Christians who believe in eternal punishment get together and decide, once and for all, whether God is unwilling or unable to help those who have died unconverted. Upon this depends whether the rational thing to do is to fear God or to love him.

Now, if we contrast all this stuff I've been talking about with Christ's attitude, well, frankly, Christ seems less authoritarian. When he lets the rich young man go, he lets him go without threats. Maybe he'll come back another day. It's all up to people to choose whether to act on what Jesus is saying, and if they choose the teaching, it's because they are attracted to it.

I want to read you something by a fellow named Maurice Nicoll, one of my heroes. He trained with Jung in Zurich, and then with Ouspensky, and finally Gurdjieff, if you know those guys. When he talks about "the Work," he means the esoteric Christianity that the group practices, but I think what he says applies to any of the sacred traditions. He says:

No meeting is possible without reciprocal affection. If the Work seeks to enter into a man's understanding, it would be unable to do so if there's nothing reciprocal coming from the man. Real conjunction with the Work needs affection before it can happen. Affection is that which opens while non-affection shuts.

And then he goes on:

If a man values many other things far more than any value he puts on the work of his inner self, it will be unable to make conjunction with him. He will not resemble that merchant seeking goodly pearls, who, when he had found one pearl of great price, went and sold all he had and bought it.

And then Nicoll says about the merchant:

Notice he had to sell first before he could buy. He sold what was valueless in comparison with the pearl. The merchant is yourself in relation to the Work. To sell means, psychologically, to get rid of former interests that you have valued by withdrawing energy from them. The released energies that you now have can go to the pearl.

In other words, (the pearl is) the sacred path or tradition that you decide to take. I love this idea that one is drawn to a teaching because of one's affection for it—that you hear the teaching and it draws affection out of you. It's impossible to *frighten* people into feeling affection. In other words, forcing people to be spiritual just doesn't work. But this isn't good enough for most organized Christianity because it does—well, it certainly used to—believe in force. First, a lot of people believe you have to choose Christianity or you go to hell. Then, consider that odd choice of the cross as the primary Christian symbol. I remember the surprise I felt the first time that a Buddhist said to me, "How extraordinary to have an instrument of torture as the central symbol of your religion."

It reminds me of *The Passion of the Christ* because the Passion is suffering. In the film, you see Jesus suffering under the direction of the diminutive and surprisingly right-wing Mel Gibson.

You see, Mel's depiction of violence is a different kind of violence. This is not terrorizing us into belief. It's putting a moral obligation on us to accept Christ's teachings because he suffered so much. We're told that Jesus suffered for us because, of course, we are sinners; he died to redeem our sins. Perhaps people are easier to control if they're feeling a bit guilty because they're sinners, particularly if the controlling force, the church, is the one that is able to declare that they *are* sinners. So the church and Mel Gibson, I think, are trying to force us to believe out of guilt.

I don't think this works psychologically because if Dick Cheney were scourged for hours and then crucified, I would genuinely feel sorry for him . . . *eventually*. The point is, it would not bring me any closer to his views. And over the centuries, some very, very, very bad people have been tortured very, very badly, but this does not make their views any better.

So what's going on here? I'm sorry to say that it reminds me of my mother because she could never give me any space within which I might feel free to *choose* to love her. She always crowded me with this network of obligations as to why I was morally obliged to love her, leaving me no space whatsoever for actual choice. You know, "After all I've done for you," or, "When I'm gone you'll be sorry," or, "I carried you for nine months." My mother's maiden name, incidentally, was Muriel Cross. Well, we all have one to bear.

Now, it seems to me that Mel and the organized churches are behaving a bit like Mum. They don't want to give us the real freedom, the real option, *not* to buy the package. It's almost as though they don't quite trust the package. They don't deep down think that it's quite good enough, you know, quite persuasive enough, so they have to sort of threaten us and manipulate us—which is where I disagree with them because I believe Christ's teaching *is* actually good enough, definitely good enough—good enough to attract our affection.

Now, compare all this violence and manipulation with what the mystics are espousing. I mean, to what extent are the mystics ordering us around and persecuting us? Not a lot. What they're prepared to tell us are a few general hints which they think might help us if we want to get closer to an experience of God. And what occurs to me is that this is something that the organized churches might be doing too if they didn't have more worldly matters on their mind.

The mystic Thomas Merton says in his book *Contemplative Prayer*: "Contemplation is essentially a listening in silence in expectancy, yet, in a certain sense, we must truly begin to hear God when we've ceased to listen." What's the meaning of this paradox? Perhaps, only that there's a higher kind of listening which is not an attentiveness to some special wavelength, a receptivity to a certain kind of message, but a general emptiness that waits for the message of God. In other words, the true contemplator is not one who prepares his mind or her mind for a particular message that he or she wants or is expecting to hear but someone who remains empty because they know that they could never expect or anticipate the word that might transform their darkness into light.

And if you go back to the 1300s, to the splendid mystic Meister Eckhart, "So, be silent and do not flap your gums about God for, to the extent that you flap your gums about God, you lie and you commit sin. Nor should you want to know anything about God because God is above our knowledge."

I love all this stuff. Sir Thomas Aquinas, whose voluminous writings probably did more to codify the teaching and doctrines of the Catholic Church than anyone else, towards the later part of his life, had a mystical experience, and he never wrote another word after that.

You see, mystics know that what is most important is ineffable. It is this lack of belief in the efficacy of words that makes it impossible to control other people, even if the mystics wanted to, which they don't. Whereas organized religion relies on words in order to exert its power over us. And if there's one thing that Christ's teaching is *not* about, it's not about power over people. Whereas organized religion is almost always about power because, unfortunately, no matter who founds the religion, eventually it nearly always falls into the hands of the power seekers.

Now, I once helped this eminent British psychiatrist Robin Skynner to write a couple of books. He was a wise old bird; he knew a thing or two. He had founded three separate psychiatric institutions in England: the Institution of Marital Therapy, the Institution of Group Analysis, and the Institute of Family Therapy. And he told me the arc of development of the institutes was always the same. At the beginning, they're formed by a small number of people who are fascinated and excited by a new body of ideas and who want to work with them and to discover what it's all about, usually for very little salary. And then a second generation comes along and they're incredibly enthusiastic because they're great admirers of the people who started it; they want to learn from the founders and also maybe to develop *their* theories a bit. But by the time you get to the fourth generation, they're all coming into the institution because of the health benefits and the promotion opportunities and the paid holidays. And that's inevitably what happens. Institutions run out of steam.

And even in the church, it means that a lot of people coming in are power seekers, whether they know it consciously or not. And power seekers, of course, rise to the top because that's what they're motivated to do. That's what they devote all their time to, while the rest of us are having dinner with friends and reading books. It gives them a huge advantage.

Eventually, the power seekers start changing the interpretation of a teaching like Christ's because they are not at a psychological or spiritual level to be able to understand it. You see, if they're told, "Love thine enemy," they think it must be some kind of trick. So, after a time, the church becomes a power-seeking institution. I mean, think of Pope Alexander VI, who had a child by his own daughter, and if anyone mentioned it, he charged them with heresy. And you can bet he thought he was justified.

Now, most of the time, most of us use religion for our own purposes. You only have to think for a moment of those ghastly expressions of serene superiority that you see on the faces of some "spiritual" people because our egos, our subconsciousnesses, are, in the end, much, much too crafty for us. Our unconsciousness can always trick us. Our ego will always get the better of us.

And, that's why we need a teacher to point out to us when our egotism is distorting the teaching because our own interpretations will probably end up serving our ego, which is, incidentally, why the Catholic Church was probably right, from the point of view of its own interests, in opposing the distribution of the Bible in the vernacular in the 1500s because everybody could then make his or her own interpretation.

And now, that leads me to another little scene from the *Life of Brian,* which teaches us, shows us, and hopefully makes us laugh at the idea of different interpretations.

*Video clip from* Life of Brian:

[Sacred music.]
FOLLOWERS: *Oh! Oh! Ohh! Oh! Ah! Oh!*
ARTHUR: *He has given us a sign!*
FOLLOWER: *Oh!*
SHOE FOLLOWER: *He has given us . . . His shoe!*
ARTHUR: *The shoe is the sign. Let us follow His example.*
SPIKE: *What?*
ARTHUR: *Let us, like Him, hold up one shoe and let the other be upon our foot, for this is His sign, that all who follow Him shall do likewise.*
EDDIE: *Yes.*
SHOE FOLLOWER: *No, no, no. The shoe is a sign that we must gather shoes together in abundance.*
GIRL: *Cast off the shoes! Follow the Gourd!*
SHOE FOLLOWER: *No! Let us gather shoes together!*
FRANK: *Yes.*
SHOE FOLLOWER: *Let me!*
ELSIE: *Oh, get off!*
YOUTH: *No, no! It is a sign that, like Him, we must think not of the things of the body, but of the face and head!*
SHOE FOLLOWER: *Give me your shoe!*
YOUTH: *Get off!*
GIRL: *Follow the Gourd! The Holy Gourd of Jerusalem!*
FOLLOWER: *The Gourd!*
HARRY: *Hold up the sandal, as He has commanded us!*
ARTHUR: *It is a shoe! It is a shoe!*
HARRY: *It's a sandal!*
ARTHUR: *No, it isn't!*
GIRL: *Cast it away!*

ARTHUR: *Put it on!*
YOUTH: *And clear off!*
SHOE FOLLOWER: *Take the shoes and follow Him!*
GIRL: *Come, . . .*
FRANK: *Yes!*
GIRL: *. . . all ye who call yourself Gourdenes!*

*End of clip.*

The history of Western Christianity there summed up in about sixty seconds.

I came across what I think is a very important idea. Now, you guys may know this, but it was new to me. It's what Robin Skynner said: "Every sacred tradition offers itself at many different levels, and the level that we take it at will be a reflection of our general level of mental health."

To give a simplified example, people at the bottom levels of mental health, and Robin thought that was about the bottom 20 percent of a population, will understand religion as a collection of rules, rewards, and punishment all enforced by a powerful and frightening God, a terrifying kind of ethereal Saddam Hussein who wants everyone to spend their time telling him how marvelous he is.

Then, as we move up the mental health scale, God begins to be seen more as the great headmaster in the sky, very stern but basically on your side. And as we continue to move up, our conception of God lofts through various forms of loving parent through to a wise friend.

And at the top level, it's much more difficult and Robin was quite clear that neither he nor I were anywhere near the top level of mental health. But at least we could read what other people who probably were (at that level) had written about it. And what he pointed out was that, at this level, God doesn't seem to be seen anymore as a person. God is experienced as a consciousness or an intelligence, an essence of love, perhaps a sense of order, even as significance or meaning. At this level, God is not an entity like a person you can do deals with when you're in trouble. Now, some of you—don't think me rude—will be somewhere in the middle of the mental health levels, where I am, so we'll tend to think of God still as a kind of person, someone with some human attributes.

I encountered this version of religion when I was growing up in England in the '50s; the Church of England offered this level, which seemed to me a bit dim even when I was only fifteen, and it kind of put me off religion for a very long time. I eventually took revenge by writing a scene for *Monty Python's The Meaning of Life*. Now, this is not from *Life of Brian*; this is from *The Meaning of Life*, and it's the chapel scene, my experience of religion at school.

*Video clip from* The Meaning of Life:

[A school chapel.]

HEADMASTER: *And spotteth twice they the camels before the third hour. And so the Midianites went forth to Ram Gilead in Kadesh Bilgemath by Shor Ethra Regalion, to the house of Gash-Bil-Betheul-Bazda, he who brought the butter dish to Balshazar and the tent peg to the house of Rashomon, and there slew they the goats, yea, and placed they the bits in little pots. Here endeth the lesson.*

[The HEADMASTER closes the Bible. The CHAPLAIN rises.]

CHAPLAIN: *Let us praise God.*

[The CONGREGATION rises.]

*Oh Lord . . .*

CONGREGATION: *Oh Lord . . .*

CHAPLAIN: *Oooh, you are so big . . .*

CONGREGATION: *Oooh, you are so big . . .*

CHAPLAIN: *So absolutely huge.*

CONGREGATION: *So ab—solutely huge.*

CHAPLAIN: *Forgive Us, O Lord, for this our dreadful toadying.*

CONGREGATION: *And barefaced flattery.*

HEADMASTER: *Amen.*

CONGREGATION: *Amen.*

HEADMASTER: *Now two boys have been found rubbing linseed oil into the school cormorant. Now some of you may feel that the cormorant does not play an important part in the life of the school but I would remind you that it was*

*presented to us by the Corporation of the town of Sudbury to commemorate*
*Empire Day, when we try to remember the names of all those from the Sud-*
*bury area who so gallantly gave their lives to keep China British. So from now*
*on the cormorant is strictly out of bounds. Oh . . . and Jenkins . . . apparently*
*your mother died this morning. [Turns to the Chaplain.] Chaplain.*
[The CONGREGATION rises and the CHAPLAIN leads them in singing.]
*CHAPLAIN AND THE CONGREGATION:*

> *Oh Lord, please don't burn us,*
> *Don't grill or toast your flock,*
> *Don't put us on the barbecue,*
> *Or simmer us in stock,*
> *Don't braise or bake or boil us,*
> *Or stir-fry us in a wok . . .*

*End of clip.*

And you know, it wasn't that much of an exaggeration.

So what we had during my time at school was Christ's teaching interpreted in the service of petit bourgeois values like respectability and prosperity and social standing, which is not, I think, what Christ was all about.

I've been listening to some tapes of Father Thomas Keating called *Contemplative Journey.* I think they're terrific. He makes the following point. He says: "Conventional Western church Christianity decrees that external acts are more important than internal motivation, that the 'self' initiates good works, that good works are rewarded here on earth and are also guarantees for future rewards in heaven." Keating says this is 180 degrees opposed to the picture that emerges from a proper study of the teachings of Christ:

1. Internal motivation is more important than external acts.
2. The spirit of God in us initiates good works, which involves us in trying to listen to God, not having our own bright ideas and expecting him to back us up.

3. No rewards for the ego but only help on the journey to unite with God and our neighbors, which involves working against the ego.

4. No guarantees about heaven, just hoping for union with God.

So, you see, where I grew up, the Christianity that was taught was the opposite of what Christ was really talking about, and nobody noticed because we disapproved of anyone who disagreed with us (because every level of mental health believes that it is the best level). Hitler did not think he was a bad man. But at least our interpretation, our Church of England interpretation of Christ's teaching, was not as intolerant and cruel as that of the people, as Robin puts it, at the very bottom levels of mental health.

Now, if we were to look at the kind of religion that appeals to those people, above all, it offers certainty. People at lower levels of mental health are very uncomfortable with ambiguity and paradox and leaving anything unresolved, any element of doubt. They like certainty and, with it, they like authority. For example, they hold, on the whole, a belief in the literal truth of the Bible, which they say has been breathed by God, despite the fact that its contents were undecided for the first four hundred years of the Christian era. And what's puzzling above all about this literal belief is that Christ taught in parables. I don't see how you can take a parable literally.

I mean, one of the best jokes in *Life of Brian* comes when Brian is actually forced, briefly, to pose as a prophet to escape from the Romans and he delivers a scrambled version of one of Christ's parables, which he's obviously heard and not understood. And he starts by saying, "There was this master who had two servants." And someone in the crowd says, "What were their names?" See, that's taking a parable literally.

And when I think of all the wise people that I've ever met, what they had in common, without exception, was a lack of literal-mindedness. They tended to think metaphorically. So it seems to me rather insulting to Christ to suggest that he is one of the literal-minded.

And further, at a low level of mental health, the fear of punishment by God for any impure, negative, destructive thoughts or feelings is so great, these thoughts are dealt by the psychological mechanism known as denial and projection. You deny that they are in *you*, of course. But you can't get rid of them by denying they are there. You still sense they're around, so you project them onto another person or another group. Then you can pretend you've got rid of all these bad feelings that are still in you. But really, you've just transferred them to the other people. So, "I'm fine, I'm pure, I'm right, all the evil is in that lot over there." You've only to look at the divisions in the world today—polarized, filled with hate talk and blame, intolerant.

Now, I just want to read you something. It's from a fundamentalist novel which I bought recently and I want to read you just a little bit of it. It's called *Glorious Appearing: The End of Days*, and it's written by two guys, Tim LaHaye and Jerry B. Jenkins. There's a picture on the back, and Tim LaHaye is the one who's had a lot of plastic surgery and whose hair is very black for a man of his age. So this is about the final battle, the final confrontation between good and evil, and the hero, who is not very important in this extract, but you'll hear his name a couple of times, is called Rayford, and he is, of course, on the Christian side. Now the Antichrist is called Nicolae Carpathia, and in the book he was, to my surprise, until recently, Secretary of the United Nations, and he reports directly to Lucifer. Presumably, as Kofi Annan does. And Carpathia heads the colossal armies of the world that have amalgamated together against the Christian army under the title of the Global Community Unity Army. Now, this is a description of the battle at the end. Everyone outside of the old city of Jerusalem are baddies, the ones that are commanded by Carpathia. Here we go:

Carpathia came into view, valiant and proud on his huge horse, sword pointing to the sky, microphone wrapped around his ear and in front of his mouth so that the entire army could hear his commands. "Horsemen, attack!" "Break through the old walls!" "Take the Temple Mount!" "Destroy the rebels!"

But when the horsemen whipped their mounts, they bolted as if blind, running headlong into the wall, throwing riders. The riders that were not thrown leapt from the horses and tried to control them with the reins, but even as they struggled, their own flesh dissolved, their eyes melted, and their tongues disintegrated.

As Rayford watched, the soldiers stood briefly as skeletons, now in baggy uniforms, and then dropped in heaps of bones as the blinded horses continued to fume and rant and rave. "Reinforcements!" Carpathia called out. "Charge! Charge! Attack!"

He lifted his sword and cursed God but, suddenly, his attention was drawn directly above. Rayford followed his gaze to see the Temple of God open in heaven and the Ark of the Covenant, as plain as day. Lightning flashed. . . . Carpathia's horse reared and high-stepped. . . . And suddenly the Lord Jesus Himself appeared in the clouds and the whole world saw him. He spoke with a loud voice saying, "Speak comfort to Jerusalem and cry out to her that her warfare is ended. . . . And that the plague with which I struck all the people who fought against Jerusalem was this: their flesh dissolved while they stood on their feet, their eyes dissolved in their sockets, and their tongues dissolved in their mouths.". . .

The Lord sat triumphant on the back of His white horse in the clouds, His army behind Him, gazing upon the one-sided victory over the forces that had come against Jerusalem.

They've sold 14 million of these books. . . .

I'm not sure where "blessed are the meek" fits in, or "love thine enemy." But, you see, this kind of stuff leaves some fundamentalists literally glowing with a sense of their own purity and moral rightness. And now that all the bad qualities of the world reside in the "out" groups, like the UN or liberals, it's a terrific feel-good experience. They feel good because they *know* they are good because all the bad things are in that lot over there.

Which is, I think, why they objected to *Life of Brian* by saying, "How could you possibly criticize us? We're Christians." Well, so was the Spanish Inquisition. And, of course, part of that sense of feeling good is the certainty that comes from being part of an authoritarian structure. Robin Skynner always pointed out to me, "Many people grow up in authoritarian families, and that feels familiar and comfortable to them; they're not comfortable with feelings of freedom and choice."

In *Life of Brian*, there's another scene where we see this tendency to conform when Brian finally addresses the crowd, who, on no good evidence, believes he is the Messiah. Actually, the previous evening, he thought he'd given them the slip and run off with his girlfriend, so it's a little bit of a surprise when he wakes up in the morning with his girlfriend, whose name is Judith (that's Judith the Scarieth), and discovers, to his alarm, that his supporters have gathered outside the window.

*Video clip from* Life of Brian:

[Rooster crows.]
*FOLLOWERS: Look! There he is! The Chosen One has woken!*
[Slam.]
[Bam, bam, bam, bam.]
*MANDY: Brian!* [Bam, bam, bam, bam, bam.]
*BRIAN: Huuh. Hooh. Ooh! Mother. Ooh. Ha—*
*MANDY: Brian!*
*BRIAN: Hang on, Mother! Shh.* [Clunk.] *Hello, Mother.*
*MANDY: Don't you "Hello, Mother" me. What are all those people doing out there?!*
*BRIAN: Oh. Well—well, I, uh—*
*MANDY: Come on! What have you been up to, my lad?!*
*BRIAN: Well, uh, I think they must have popped by for something.*
*MANDY: Popped by?! Swarmed by, more like! There's a multitude out there!*
*BRIAN: Mm, they—they started following me yesterday.*
*MANDY: Well, they can stop following you right now. Now, stop following my son! You ought to be ashamed of yourselves.*
*FOLLOWERS: The Messiah! The Messiah! Show us the Messiah!*
*MANDY: The who?*
*FOLLOWERS: The Messiah!*

MANDY: Huh, there's no Messiah in here. There's a mess, all right, but no Messiah.
    Now, go away!

FOLLOWERS: Brian! Brian!

MANDY: Right, my lad. What have you been up to?

BRIAN: Nothing, Mum. Um—

MANDY: Come on. Out with it.

BRIAN: Well, they think I'm the Messiah, Mum.

MANDY: [Smacks him.] Now, what have you been telling them?

BRIAN: Nothing! I only—

MANDY: You're only making it worse for yourself.

BRIAN: Look! I can explain! I—

[Smack.]

JUDITH: No! Let me explain, Mrs. Cohen!

MANDY: Who—

JUDITH: Your son is a born leader. Those people out there are following him because
    they believe in him, Mrs. Cohen. They believe he can give them hope—hope of
    a new life, a new world, a better future!

MANDY: Who's that?!

BRIAN: Oh! . . . Judith, Mum. Judith. Mother. Hmm. [Smack.] Aaaah!

FOLLOWERS: The Messiah! The Messiah!

MANDY: Ooooh.

FOLLOWERS: Show us the Messiah! The Messiah! The Messiah! Show us the
    Messiah!

MANDY: Now, you listen here! He's not the Messiah. He's a very naughty boy!
    Now, go away!

FOLLOWERS: Who are you?!

MANDY: I'm his mother. That's who.

FOLLOWERS: Behold his mother! Behold his mother!

MANDY: Ohhh, now, don't think you can get around me like that. Did you hear
    what I said?

FOLLOWERS: Yes!

MANDY: Oh, I see. It's like that, is it?

FOLLOWERS: Yes!

MANDY: Ohh. Oh, all right, then. You can see him for one minute, but not one
    second more. Do you understand?

FOLLOWERS: Yes.

MANDY: *Promise?*

FOLLOWERS: *Well, all right. Brian! Brian! Brian!*

BRIAN: *Good morning.*

FOLLOWERS: *A blessing! A blessing! A blessing!*

BRIAN: *No. No, please! Please! Please listen. I've got one or two things to say.*

FOLLOWERS: *Tell us. Tell us both of them.*

BRIAN: *Look. You've got it all wrong. You don't need to follow me. You don't need to follow anybody! You've got to think for yourselves. You're all individuals!*

FOLLOWERS: *Yes, we're all individuals!*

BRIAN: *You're all different!*

FOLLOWERS: *Yes, we are all different!*

DENNIS: *I'm not.*

ARTHUR: *Shhhh.*

FOLLOWERS: *Shh. Shhh. Shhh.*

BRIAN: *You've all got to work it out for yourselves!*

FOLLOWERS: *Yes! We've got to work it out for ourselves!*

BRIAN: *Exactly!*

FOLLOWERS: *Tell us more!*

BRIAN: *No! That's the point! Don't let anyone tell you what to do! Otherwise—Ow! No!*

MANDY: *Come on, Brian. That's enough. That's enough.*

FOLLOWERS: *Oooooh. That wasn't a minute!*

MANDY: *Oh, yes, it was.*

FOLLOWERS: *Oh, no, it wasn't!*

MANDY: *Now, stop that, and go away!*

YOUTH: *Excuse me.*

MANDY: *Yes?*

YOUTH: *Are you a virgin?*

MANDY: *I beg your pardon!*

YOUTH: *Well, if it's not a personal question, are you a virgin?*

MANDY: *If it's not a personal question? How much more personal can you get? Now, piss off!*

*End of clip.*

I'm glad you laughed at that line when they all chorus, "We're all individuals," and one guy says, "I'm not."

Well, I've gone on long enough. Let me just summarize very, very quickly what Robin says about the interpretations of the teachings. At the bottom level, Christ's teachings are seen as extremely important rules which must be kept precisely because focusing on the letter of the law, rather than the spirit of the law, is characteristic of behavior at lower levels of mental health. At the middle level of mental health, people pay more attention to the spirit than they do to the letter of the law.

And at the top level, if anyone's interested, there's a particular book by Maurice Nicoll called *The New Man*, in which he goes through Christ's parables and explains them in terms of psychological information. So we can read these and understand better how our minds work and what we need to do to make our minds work differently if we are ever to be transformed or reborn. We're helped to "repent" in its real meaning of "rethink."

So, that's where I'm going to finish, but I think we can manage two or three questions.

STUDENT: I've known a good number of religious people, many of whom approached religion basically from a mystical perspective and many of whom approached it from a legalistic, heavy-handed perspective. And I've got to say, both categories of worshippers always struck me as on a pretty low level of mental health. So I'm wondering what basis you have for differentiating a scale of approaching God.

JOHN CLEESE: Well, I'm relying really on Robin Skynner. He was an exceptionally good and famous psychiatrist and, unlike most psychiatrists, he spent his life studying what constitutes *good* mental health. If you actually think of it, most psychiatrists base their whole body of teaching on examples of fairly bad health. It's rather as though if you were writing a book about how to play golf, you'd go and study the twenty-five worst golfers in your district and figure out from that how you could become a really good golfer.

Robin was not like that. Robin was fascinated by various studies; one study, in particular, done by Robert Beavers and his team at Timberlawn psychiatric hospital in Dallas, found that healthy families share many of the same characteristics. And Robin figured out how various levels of mental health operated and the characteristic behaviors of all of them.

Now, once he'd done that, because he was also interested in religion, he basically correlated what he saw was different people's approach to religion with the levels of mental health as he understood them. Not to say that we're always at one level. If we're very stressed, our level will drop, and if we'd had a nice three-week holiday and got on well with everyone, our level will go up. But generally, we operate pretty much on the same level.

All I can say is, the people that I know who are more interested in experiential religion seem to be much more relaxed, very kind to people, and much easier to talk to about important matters because they aren't trying to defend their experience.

STUDENT: I was just wondering, you mentioned the concept of hell as a scare tactic and I know, a few years ago, the Vatican released a statement that they no longer believed that hell was some burning inferno of torture but was, instead, a state of being, a spiritual state that was completely displaced from God, instead of a physical torture place. I wonder what your opinion was of this.

CLEESE: Well, I've read a certain amount about people who have had visions, psychedelic experiences, and it seems to me there's no question at all that, when they have a bad experience, their visions are very akin to pictures of hell like Hieronymus Bosch painted, that kind of thing. So I believe that it is very possible for us to be in hell in the sense that we are feeling absolutely terrible and we are having very frightening visions. But that, I think, is in our minds. I think the greatest mistake that is made in religion is to take literally what is intended metaphorically. I think the people who had these experiences thought they had seen something *real*, whereas all they'd done is to have an experience in their own mind. So that's where the idea of hell came from. But there's no question at all that a lot of people believe in hell as a physical reality. I was talking to a rabbi six or seven weeks ago who'd been on a panel in the South talking to an audience of fundamentalists and he, very nicely, with great humor, he actually confronted them and he said, "You do believe that I'm going to burn in hell in eternity. Don't you?" They didn't like to say it, but that's what they believed. So although the Catholics may have transmuted hell into a more metaphorical state, which I think is correct, the number of people who still believe in hell as a punishment for sinners and for those who do not share their beliefs, basically, is very large.

STUDENT: I actually have two questions. The first one is, what do you think about people flying planes into buildings or put a bomb on their back and claim it's in the name of God? The second question is kind of hard for me to explain, but there are a lot of people who I know who market themselves as very religious, following a particular religion, but they happen to disagree with a lot of elements of it. My question is this: if you really don't agree with it, then why bother being in that religion? Why don't you, basically, create your own, which is kind of like what I'm doing. I used to be Catholic, but I'm not so much anymore.

CLEESE: Okay. So far as 9/11 is concerned, I don't know what one could say about that. It was a group of lunatics, of extreme fundamentalists doing something unspeakably wicked. What more can one say?

So far as the other goes, I do believe that there *is* something out there. I'm not sure what it is. And if you think there might be something out there, even if you don't know what, you will find, if you sniff around, *something* that's interesting. I started with a book called *Tao: The Watercourse Way*, by Alan Watts. I remember reading it and thinking, "What the hell is this about?" It was a description of Taoism, a Chinese religion, and that got me started.

The problem about starting your own religion is that your ego will always trick you. Eventually, your ego will have you rewarding your ego while pretending to be religious, and that's why, I think, some of the finest people I've ever met come from the contemplative tradition where they have some kind of teacher because, when you talk to your teacher, he or she can say, "Ah, ha. Wait a moment. This is your ego. This is what it's up to." Your teacher can show you what your ego's doing because your unconscious is much, much cleverer than you think.

STUDENT: I just wondered if you could speak a little bit about the face of secularism in America.

CLEESE: Well, Robin Skynner, from whom I learned almost everything useful, said that he felt that there were two stages that people in his therapy group exhibited as they were beginning to get happier. (I was a patient in his group for about three and a half years, a group of about eight people.)

The first is they start laughing at their own behavior. Robin said that means they're about two-thirds of the way there. They're going to be okay. When they actually look at their own behavior and they realize, "There I go again." They recognize that little bit of space between whatever it is that *observes* our behavior and the behavior itself, and they start responding to it with a little bit of humor.

The second stage is belief in something that's bigger than yourself. If you have some kind of belief system in which you're a part of something that's larger than you, then you're on the surface of something that's bigger than your own egotistical desires. For some of you, organized religion may fit the bill. But Robin felt that, unless there is something greater than *you* that you subscribe to, you are always going to stay at a lower, narrower, more selfish level and be less happy as a result.

I'm going to go away. Thank you. Bye.

*Video clip from* Life of Brian:

MR. FRISBEE: *Cheer up, Brian. You know what they say.*
*Some things in life are bad.*
*They can really make you mad.*

*Other things just make you swear and curse.*
*When you're chewing on life's gristle,*
*Don't grumble. Give a whistle.*
*And this'll help things turn out for the best.*
*And . . .*
[Music.]
*Always look on the bright side of life.*
[Whistling.]
*Always look on the light side of life.*
[Whistling.]
*If life seems jolly rotten,*
*There's something you've forgotten,*
*And that's to laugh and smile and dance and sing.*
*When you're feeling in the dumps,*
*Don't be silly chumps.*
*Just purse your lips and whistle. That's the thing.*
*And . . .*
*Always look on the bright side of life.*
SEVERAL: [Whistling.]
MR. FRISBEE: Come on!
SEVERAL: *Always look on the right side of life,*
[Whistling.]
MR. FRISBEE: *For life is quite absurd*
*And death's the final word.*
*You must always face the curtain with a bow.*
*Forget about your sin.*
*Give the audience a grin.*
EVERYONE: *Enjoy it. It's your last chance, anyhow.*
*So . . .*
*Always look on the bright side of death,*
[Whistling.]
*Just before you draw your terminal breath.*
[Whistling.]
MR. FRISBEE: *Life's a piece of shit,*

*When you look at it.*

*Life's a laugh and death's a joke. It's true.*

*You'll see it's all a show.*

*Keep 'em laughing as you go.*

*Just remember that the last laugh is on you.*

*And . . .*

*EVERYONE: Always look on the bright side of life.*

[Whistling.]

*Always look on the right side of life.*

[Whistling.]

*MR. FRISBEE: Come on, Brian. Cheer up.*

*EVERYONE: Always look on the bright side of life!*

[Whistling.]

*Always look on the bright side of life!*

[Whistling.]

*MR. FRISBEE: Worse things happen at sea, you know.*

*EVERYONE: Always look on the bright side of life!*

*MR. FRISBEE: I mean, what you got to lose? You know, you come from nothing.*

*EVERYONE: [Whistling.]*

*MR. FRISBEE: You're going back to nothing. What have you lost? Nothing!*

*EVERYONE: Always look on the bright side of life!*

[Whistling.]

*MR. FRISBEE: Nothing will come from nothing. You know what they say?*

*EVERYONE: Always look on the bright side of life!*

*MR. FRISBEE: Cheer up, you old bugger. Come on. Give us a grin. There you*
    *are. See?*

*EVERYONE: [Whistling.]*

*MR. FRISBEE: It's the end of the film. Incidentally, this record's available in the*
    *foyer.*

*EVERYONE: Always look on the bright side of life!*

*MR. FRISBEE: Some of us have got to live as well, you know.*

*EVERYONE: [Whistling.]*

*MR. FRISBEE: Who do you think pays for all this rubbish?*

*EVERYONE: Always look on the bright side of life!*

# CREATIVITY, GROUP DYNAMICS, AND CELEBRITY

## JOHN CLEESE AND BETA MANNIX

APRIL 19, 2009

PROVOST KENT FUCHS: Welcome. I'm Cornell Provost Kent Fuchs, and it is wonderful to have so many of you here as an enthusiastic crowd.

This event marks a decade of formal association between John Cleese and Cornell. He has visited campus every year for the past ten years and brought us new insights and new ways of looking at the world, as well as innovative ways of teaching and communicating. He is part comedian, part psychologist, part master teacher, and fully a public intellectual.

Today, John Cleese is teaming up with a member of our own faculty, Elizabeth (Beta) Mannix, who is the Ann Whitney Olin Professor of Management and vice provost for equity and inclusion. Her research, teaching, and her interests in that area include effective performance in managerial teams, diversity in organizations and teams, power and alliances, and organizational change and renewal.

So please now welcome Mr. Cleese and also Beta Mannix.

BETA MANNIX: Thank you, John, for being here. Since we are at a university, I thought I would start with a little of your university life and schooling. I've done a little research on that, as you know. You told me you weren't a high-tech person.

JOHN CLEESE: Oh, I'm completely . . . the joke about being Q in the Bond movies is that, when I did it the first time, I wasn't Q; I was R because Desmond Llewelyn, who was Q in seventeen of those movies, had said to the Bond people he felt that he needed an assistant. So it was his suggestion I should come in, and I was there talking to him and to Pierce Brosnan, and we were all in fits of laughter about the fact we are all absolutely hopeless at technology. And here we were, you know, as the gadget-meisters handing things over to Bond, and not one of us had the slightest idea how any of it worked. Yes—not strong on modern technology.

MANNIX: Let me ask you a little bit about how you got started doing what you're doing, which wasn't a particularly straight path. You started off in going to a fairly well-respected prep school and you took your A levels, which we think of as sort of advanced tests, in things like mathematics, physics, and chemistry. You taught science. You told me just today you taught history. You went to Cambridge. You read law. You have a degree in law. And then, life took sort of a different route for you.

CLEESE: Well, how many people really know what they want to do?

MANNIX: I don't know. I think some of these kids *do* know; I think some really do.

CLEESE: Put your hand up if you really think at this stage you know what you want to do with your life. You see, what is it? What is it, one in five? Is it 5 percent? It's just over 5 percent. I've always been amazed that some people know what they want to do.

A lot of my heroes are people who just decided to do something. For example, I have a connection with a wonderful conservation zoo on the small island of Jersey. Actually, it really should be French—it's off the coast of France—but it's English. A guy called Gerry Durrell started a conservation zoo there, which is now the model for most of the conservation zoos in the world. Gerry *always* knew that was what he wanted to do, even as a child, and I think it's amazing when somebody knows and just goes for it.

And I have a friend in London called Bryan Magee, who is a philosopher, and he always, *always* was fascinated by philosophy. But he didn't want to become a member of a university philosophy department because he said if you do that, you have to keep up with every current trend in philosophy, and he thinks a lot of them are not worth keeping up with. So he became a broadcaster who talks about philosophy. But he's done that all his life. I had lunch with him three weeks ago. He's now in his late seventies. Here's a guy who *knew* what he wanted to do. And I find that wonderful.

But I have never known what I want to do. All I know is that I want to do the next project. Do you see what I mean?

I think, deep down, psychology has always been my fascination. When I was fifteen or sixteen, I saw a few documentaries on BBC television that were about psychology and I can still remember some of them. There was one in which a cat was offered a saucer of milk and a saucer of alcohol. And, of course, it drank the milk and ignored the alcohol. Then, they deliberately did things to frustrate it. It started drinking the alcohol.

There was another documentary where somebody was hypnotized, and he was told that, when the hypnotist returned to the room, he should go to a vase of flowers, take the flowers out of the vase, and pour the water on the floor. And that's exactly what happened. The hypnotist walked in, the guy went over to the vase, he took the flowers out of the vase, and he poured the water on the floor. When questioned, "Why did you do that?" he said, "Um . . . I, I think, I sort of thought I saw some smoke there and I thought someone had dropped a cigarette." And it was quite clear to me that he was making it up. He had no idea why he'd poured the water out. And that fascinated me.

That was my first experience of rationalization. So I wanted to know about psychology. At school, I went in the biology group and the teaching was *terrible*. Dr. Davy—I mean, just hopeless.

MANNIX: You're going to call him out.

CLEESE: I'm going to call out his name: Dr. Davy. And Stubbs was the other guy. And there was another teacher called Lindsey Jones, who everyone, of course, called "Flimsy Bones," who taught physics.

And at the end of the first term, I came fourth in quite a large class in physics and you'd think that was okay. Okay? Now I'll tell you I came fourth with 27 percent! I knew I was in trouble. So I switched from the physics class, got my A levels, got into Cambridge on science, but wasn't deeply interested.

I had to switch to law because there was almost nothing else I could switch to.

MANNIX: So, you're saying law is easier?

CLEESE: Well, law was kind of easier for me because I am fairly precise with my use of words and I can think in terms of categories, which is all law is—until you start practicing, and then it's about villainy and low cunning.

I'll tell you my favorite joke about lawyers because it actually involves universities. The psychological departments of universities are using lawyers now, instead of rats, in their experiments. There are three reasons for this. One is that there are more lawyers than rats. Second, there are some things that rats just won't do. And the third is that there was a bit of a problem because sometimes the experimenters got fond of the rats. And I want you to know that telling you that joke has got nothing to do with the fact that I am going through an expensive divorce at the moment.

MANNIX: No.

CLEESE: So the point is I was fascinated by psychology, but it wasn't for about twenty-five years that I was able to get back to it by a circuitous route.

MANNIX: I want to talk with you about that in a bit because, when you come to Cornell, you certainly spend a lot of time talking to psychologists. It comes up throughout your entire career, I think.

CLEESE: Well, psychology fascinates me. I think the most interesting thing in the world is how this thing works [*pointing to his head*] and why we do the things we do.

MANNIX: Let me come back to the writing for a minute. I want to come back to the psychology piece of it too because, in your writing, I think it informs your writing. When you decided law wasn't for you, you went to write for the BBC. So much of your work is writing, really.

CLEESE: Yes.

MANNIX: I think a lot of people know you as an actor, but I'd say much of your work is about writing.

CLEESE: That's right. I always think of myself as a writer-performer. In other words, I write the thing and then I perform it. But for me, the interesting bit is writing it.

MANNIX: I see that a lot in what you do. What's interesting to me, too—you've talked about this—some of the earliest work you did was with Monty Python—Graham Chapman, Michael Palin, Eric Idle, and the Terrys—and you've really made no secret that you were not necessarily one big happy group of guys.

CLEESE: Well, that's right. That's right.

MANNIX: You really didn't get along that well.

CLEESE: Well, think about it. You can all think of bands, and how many of them have stayed together? A very special, select group. But on the whole, they break up because there are always tensions in any group of human beings—there's always some degree of tension. Diversity often means conflict.

And that's why I know Beta Mannix, because I'm fascinated by the way people work in groups. She's taught me an awful lot about her research in how people interact, particularly creatively.

So it's interesting that we are talking about the Python group because the funny thing was that it was democracy gone mad. I mean, no one was in charge, and it is very unusual, I think, to get a good group of people working together satisfactorily when no one is in charge.

MANNIX: Do you think that it made people better, because it seems that you did play a lot of times to your strengths?

CLEESE: Yes.

MANNIX: I think about some of the characters that you played oftentimes. You obviously are brilliant at physical comedy. And I'm sure

I'm not the first person who's noticed you often played the angrier person in the group—with a sort of seething rage that's bound to burst out.

CLEESE: Well, I think the English are terribly funny when they're angry because they absolutely don't know how to do it.

There's an episode— Connie, who was my first wife, is American. In fact, most of my wives have been American, as far as I can remember. Connie and I wrote an episode called "Waldorf Salad," if you know that one, which is all about the fact that Americans know how to complain and the British don't. The British just sit there, as happens in that episode, saying, "Isn't it awful?" and, "This food is dreadful," and, "They haven't cooked the potatoes." And somebody comes up and asks, "Is everything all right?" "Very nice, indeed, thank you." All they then do is never come back.

The English are very, very poor at complaining. They equate being angry with losing their temper. And it's absolutely nothing to do with losing one's temper. Anger is a kind of energy, which, if you can control it, gets a lot done. If you lose your temper, you dissipate the anger and make a bit of a fool of yourself. In England, to be angry, to lose one's temper, is almost a loss of face. It's very strange, a huge cultural difference.

MANNIX: When you talk about Monty Python, you talk about democracy gone mad. Was there somebody who eventually was able to take control of that group to make the decisions?

CLEESE: No.

MANNIX: How did you decide? Was it you?

CLEESE: Well, what really happened was that there were two people in the group who were slightly dominant. There was me and there was Terry Jones. And Terry Jones is small and dark and Welsh and a bit hairy. The problem with Terry is that he simply does not understand that the Welsh are a subject race who God put upon the planet to carry out menial tasks for the English. Now, why he doesn't get that, I simply don't know. It's beyond me, but it was always sort of a bone of contention. But seriously, he and I used to lock horns and disagree on almost everything because I was sort of snotty and superior and using sort of a cold, rather sarcastic intellect. And he was all Welsh fervor. He felt strongly about absolutely everything, which infuriated me because I didn't mind him feeling strongly about some things, but he felt strongly about *everything*, and he had to have his way about *everything*. So we would lock horns and the other four, to switch analogy, would get on the scales and, because we were balancing each other out, the others would get on and then the majority view could pretty much prevail.

The extraordinary thing was, if you want to understand the Python group, we were six writers who performed our own material. All the squabbles and fights were about the material. They were never about the casting. Which is weird, isn't it? Because you'd think we'd each want the best part—but we didn't. Once we'd written the material, we knew perfectly well that Graham should play that, Michael should play that . . . it was obvious to us.

MANNIX: To go back to your education in science and law, and I think you studied religion as well, right? Were all those things important pieces in your ability to write these unbelievably hysterically funny sketches? Where did all that come from? Or was it just a waste—was the education just a waste?

CLEESE: No, no, no.

MANNIX: I *hoped* you were going to say no.

CLEESE: No, it *did* teach me to think, but when you look back on it and see what you learned—for example, take trigonometry. It may have been reasonably good for training my mind, but remembering that the sine is the perpendicular of the hypotenuse and all that kind of thing was not of great value to me in my later life.

And I was taught absolutely nothing about, for example, aspects of religion which I find really fascinating, such as mysticism, which, after all, is what the founders of most religions were—mystics. This is something that is completely ignored when religion is taught because it is made into an intellectual theory, where really it starts with experience.

I was not taught anything about health or about how the human body worked, which would have been really useful. I was taught nothing about psychology, which would have been fascinating. But, you know, there was a curriculum—some of it was useful and some of it wasn't—and I think it needs to be revised a lot. But the important thing was that I was taught to think analytically.

But the interesting thing, Beta Mannix, and *you* would know this, is that if anyone wants to get into an MBA program, all the questions that they're asked to see whether they are qualified to enter this splendid program, whatever or wherever it is, all those questions are about critical analytical thinking. There will not be a single question to test your creativity. And yet, if you think of all the people who have really made a difference, like Edison, Einstein, Steve Jobs—these are people who were immensely creative. Now, why would it be that you can get into an MBA program without anyone testing your creativity or making any attempt to suggest how you could become more creative? Do you realize how insane that is? You see what I mean? It's a terrible, insane blind spot.

MANNIX: So where do you learn that? How did *you* learn that?

CLEESE: Well, I learned it because when I was at Cambridge, there was a club called the Footlights, which is like the Hasty Pudding at Harvard, and I joined it. There was no drama department at Cambridge at all. You see, I've never had a drama lesson in my life. I've simply watched people who were good and stolen from them! Seriously. So there was a very interesting mix—there were classicists and historians and scientists and engineers. They weren't all English people. It was fascinating. And there was also a mixture of social classes. We had one or two lords and several people from very poor working-class homes. And they'd all come into this clubroom where you could get lunch and a drink in the evening, and there was a little stage about half the size of this. And I *loved* being there. The price of being a member was that you had to produce a sketch and perform in it now and again. It was there I discovered that, if I was given a sheet of paper, I could sit down and after two and a half hours I would have written something which had a very good chance of making people laugh. I suddenly discovered that I had this creative ability.

And yet, my entire education from the age of six to twenty-four—I was very old when I left Cambridge—I went through that entire period without a single teacher ever telling me that I was, in any way, creative. I think the problem with the educational system is that, by and large, kids are allowed to paint when they are young, but after that stops, it's all about developing what you can refer to as the left brain, and very little of it is about the right brain. I believe that a pretty happy and successful life has to do with getting a balance between the two.

To go right back to your question of about twenty-five minutes ago, I think the reason that I've been successful as a writer is that I can be creative but I've also got a critical mind, so that when I've come up with stuff using my creative side, I can then analyze it and figure out what works and what doesn't, using my analytical side.

MANNIX: Where does criticism play into this? Recently you've taken on, I believe, the title of contributing editor at *The Spectator*, a very well-respected British magazine. You wrote an article (Google it if you haven't seen it), which talks about some scathing criticism you had in your career, and it was not helpful criticism.

CLEESE: No.

MANNIX: It was mean-spirited criticism.

CLEESE: But it was very funny to be asked to write for this magazine, which had never given me a good review in thirty years. So my first piece was actually quoting all these horrible reviews.

MANNIX: Nasty. But there's a difference between useful criticism that you want to take onboard and makes you think, I'm going to make some changes as a result of this . . .

CLEESE: Yes.

MANNIX: . . . and mean-spirited criticism. But, as you also say, you need the ability to have self-reflection and internal criticism.

CLEESE: Well, you see, the great thing about being in the Python group was that the group was really, really good on scripts. And they were also pretty good on performing. So if you read a script out to that group and they laughed at some of it and didn't laugh at other bits, well . . . it was hard to find better criticism. The Pythons would say, "This is strong." "Why don't you do this?" "We'll do that." "I don't think that works." The feedback was phenomenal. And I think we need that. In fact, I have a speech that I do to business groups in which I say: "Isn't it terrific guided missiles get so much criticism?" The reason I say this silly thing is that guided missiles every moment are sending out signals asking, "Am I on target?" And they are constantly getting signals back saying, "No, slow down a bit and a foot to the left." And they're doing that all the time.

A lot of us are so sensitive to criticism that we don't want people criticizing us, *ever*. Criticism has got to be offered in a supportive and friendly way: "I'm on your side, but wouldn't it be better if . . ." Do you see what I mean? And a lot of the time, I think, when criticism is offered, it comes out of anxiety and people are immediately focusing on what's wrong and needs to be fixed. Whereas any time that you're giving someone feedback about something, the first thing is to try to find some positive things you can say: "Really, this is good. It can be better, but it's worth working on. Well done." This is how, I think, you can make it better. And if you put criticism within that framework, then people can hear it. But if you immediately start off by saying, "Well, this is wrong and this is wrong," then the shutters go up because we all have very fragile egos. I'm sorry, but our egos are very fragile and in order to take criticism, it has to be offered in the right way.

MANNIX: That makes sense. It's something that we can all take on. It's important. I'm interested to know, is it harder for people to be critical of you, or do you find it harder to get good criticism now that you are, let's face it, famous?

CLEESE: Yes. People are too impressed in this country by fame. There's a kind of reverence which is really quite sickening. It's the opposite in England because, in England, if you are very famous, everyone is envious of you. If you want to be really popular in England, have a big public failure. Nobody feels envious, and they can all feel really good about themselves because they come to your rescue and show that they are still your friend despite the fact that you're a terrible failure.

Here, there's a big problem getting feedback. If I show a movie and I ask the audience afterwards, "What do you not like about the movie?" they won't say anything. I have to phrase it very, very positively. I say, "If I'm going to edit that film and show it again tomorrow, what two or three things can I do to make it better?" Then they'll tell me. Do you see what I mean? You have to phrase it in this way.

People don't like offering criticism. How many times have you said to any of your very good friends, "You really need to look at this aspect of your behavior"? So that's what I'm saying about criticism. It's much harder to get good criticism than you think, and it's very important when you give criticism that you give it in a positive context.

MANNIX: I've seen you interviewed, especially before the election of President Obama, and you were certainly very, very positive about Barack Obama. Very supportive. One of the things I've heard you say about him and about the election, about politics in general, is disappointment about our inability to elect a president in this country who is intellectually superior, or at least somebody who is *smart*. I think that is also related to this idea of open communication and frankness, the ability to talk about what's important, and that's about feedback too. That's about being able to talk about important issues, isn't it? And what was surprising during the interview was that you were angry about it.

CLEESE: I *was* angry. I have to tell you about a strange coincidence today. I went on Keith Olbermann—I think it was the Friday before the election—because I really wanted people to know about that remark John McCain made in front of a large audience; he had referred to Americans as "my fellow prisoners." I thought it was one of the funniest things I had ever heard in my life. I spent a long time thinking, what else could you say that would be as much a giveaway as "my fellow prisoners"? This afternoon I was taking exercise in the gym here at the Statler, and I switched on the television and there was Bill Maher. And out comes Keith Olbermann, and what I loved about Keith was that he was getting angry.

I think the problem in America is that you have a head of state who is also the top political guy. You see, in England, we have a queen who is separate from the prime minister, and this means we can be quite rude to the prime minister without insulting the figurehead of the nation. Your problem is that you are much too respectful of the president. I mean, George Bush would not have gotten away with a single one of those press conferences in the UK because the press would have sniffed out the fact that he was inadequate. He's oftentimes just *rambling*. You know, he'd start off with something—it was like listening to Sarah Palin—you don't know *where* they're going!

I mean, it's pathetic. And here he is representing what is the most important country of the world. Can you imagine what the rest of the world thought? It's embarrassing because we *want* America to be great. I felt a touch emotional when I said that because in the '60s, we *looked up* to America. It was the beacon. It was a smart place. We loved that because everybody wants a good role model, you know. I was so sick of English politics at that time and it was marvelous to see somebody like Kennedy come in; suddenly the president was being smart. It was cool to be bright. And that was wonderful. And then you have eight years of this . . . rubbish. What the British are saying now is, "Where's the American sense of *outrage*?" You know? Because it *does* matter.

MANNIX: Do you have hopes for us now?

CLEESE: Yes, I do, because I think Obama's very bright, more than bright. There are a lot of bright people, but I think he is astonishingly emotionally intelligent.

MANNIX: You like to talk emotion. You're really interested in this connection. I think you think it's lacking. You have done work in which you talk about the connection between doctors and their patients, between managers and their employees and the lack of communication, a lack of connection which gets down to this lack of emotion and the willingness to express the appropriate emotion.

CLEESE: Flexibility and openness and all those things.

MANNIX: Why is that so hard for people? Americans like to think that we're good at this, that we're open, that we're frank, that we're able to do this. But we're not, really, are we?

CLEESE: Well, I don't know. I think in the '60s you were. I think there was much more openness and much more clarity and much more freedom of communication.

You see, the English are very uncomfortable with emotion. They just don't like it. It makes them uncomfortable. For a long time the whole society in England was based on, "We've got an empire to run; we don't have time to be depressed." We were a terrible bunch of rogues through the 1700s. We were a bunch of rip-off people—we were buccaneers and cheats—and we were very entrepreneurial.

Then, suddenly, we found we had an empire, and all of a sudden everybody started wearing gray. We didn't wear gray until we had an empire; we started putting on hats, stovepipe hats, and started taking ourselves very seriously. I think you can have a society that's serious without solemnity. You see, solemnity is a particular sort of face that you put on. Well, sometimes it's appropriate, like public funerals. When some great president or a prime minister, or when a crowned head has died, it's absolutely right to have a proper ceremony in which people are not sitting on whoopee cushions. We can behave with respect in public on those occasions. But the rest of the time, what's the point of solemnity?

And we can have a very serious discussion about our kid's education, or something like that, and still be laughing. So there's a way where you can have a nice *flow* of ideas and a simplicity of emotion and we can explore different feelings without the thing having a monotonous tone to it. Do you see what I mean?

MANNIX: Some of your Video Arts films are concerned with management essentials. You tackle subjects like coaching and assertiveness and how to deliver bad news. These are skills that managers should have, and you demonstrate them with humor.

CLEESE: Yes, for example, one of the things that I've learned that really works is, if you have bad news to give someone in an interview or in a situation like that, give it right up front. Don't beat about the bush for twenty-five minutes, because they sense that something's up and become more and more anxious. Tell them the bad news. You know, if you've got to fire someone, then *say* it and then give them a chance to be a bit emotional, which is actually reasonable, and then as they come out of the emotion, you can start discussing how you'll handle it and what to do about it.

In England, we had terrible industrial relations for years. In the past, the directors of the company—the fat cats—would stick a notice on the board at three o'clock on Friday afternoon, get in their cars, and drive off to the golf course. You see what I mean? Refusing any kind of ordinary human interaction. If you behave properly with people and just treat them as proper human beings, they can take bad news.

You know what's the worst thing you can do to kids? It's to *lie* to them. Robin Skynner, with whom I wrote those books, said that kids are unbelievably resilient, providing they're not lied to.

And I didn't feel that was the case in the last eight years. I mean, who's going to be open with Cheney? What's the point? And these people *know* it. Rumsfeld used to start his big meetings at the Pentagon by saying, "Who's buying?" Meaning, who is going to pay for this? Who wants this meeting? That's a great start, isn't it? Who wants this meeting? This is somebody who really won't listen to a new idea because they've got completely stuck. Unlike the guided missile, they're not listening to any feedback.

Now Obama gets into office and he puts in people with different ideas and wants to have a good argument. *That's* how you make things exciting and vibrant, not with a bunch of know-it-alls at the top who are treating all the people under them as second-class citizens who have got to do what they are told. Somebody once said, "Why not use the intelligence of the entire organization instead of just using the intelligence of the CEO and having everyone else just carry out his ideas?"

MANNIX: This really cycles back to your interest in psychology. A lot of what you've done from the very beginning has been about learning, bringing in new ideas, and constantly doing something new as you go. The thing that's fascinating is that you never said, "I am going to be a writer, I am going to be an actor, I'm going to stop here and that's good enough." You have gone on—you name it: you've been a producer, you've been a director, you've been a writer of not only screenplays but of books.

CLEESE: Well, people go on about that, but I have also never done anything brave. I've never been in the armed forces. I am hopeless musically. I have a bad visual sense. I have no visual memory. I can't think in three dimensions.

MANNIX: You have a long list . . . rather, of the things that you just said—these are the things I'm great at, these are the things I'm not really great at. Is there a list where you say, I just want to keep trying, I have a short attention span?

CLEESE: I figure I *do* have a short attention span because when I've done something and done it reasonably well for a bit, I want to do something else. In my last year at Cambridge, we did this show in the local professional theater in town, and it was supposed to last two weeks and then we were all supposed to go off and be, in my case, a lawyer, or a teacher or work in advertising.

And all of a sudden there were people there saying, "Do you want to come and work for the BBC?" and, "We would like to take your show and put it on in the West End," which I'm sure you know, is the British equivalent of Broadway. And so, I got into entertainment completely by accident.

But to answer your question, after six weeks of doing that show, I had a week of being crazy with boredom because I'd done every single sketch in that show as well as I could. And the seventh week, I thought, "Well, what do I do now? Go out, and do everything slightly less well?" You see what I mean? It kind of depressed me, and I realized after a time that you just have to take pride in making it as good as you can each night. It can't go on getting better, really. You can keep it fresh, but it doesn't go on getting better, which it has up to that time, because it takes you six weeks to figure out how to play with it, how to make everything work.

Because of that, after we'd done two series of *Monty Python*, I thought we were repeating ourselves and that we were taking bits of sketches and putting them together, that we were just permutating and combining and not coming up with anything new. In fact, in the third series, there were only two sketches that I thought were genuinely original. The other Pythons, it seemed to my mind, were just having a good time and they just didn't *hear* me say, "What's the point of doing this if we're not being original, if we're not creating something new?" So that's basically why I split.

But there was another reason why I split, and that was that Graham Chapman, between the beginning of *Monty Python* in '69 and the time I left in '73, had become a fully fledged alcoholic and nobody else wanted to work with him.

MANNIX: That would be difficult.

CLEESE: Yeah.

MANNIX: I've seen your eulogy of Graham Chapman.

CLEESE: Have you seen that?

MANNIX: [*To audience*] You should wander around YouTube and see the eulogy.

Let me ask one final question, and then I'm going to ask the audience for questions. I have to say it's something I promised my husband, who is somewhere here in the audience. One of his favorite movies of all time is *The Magic Christian*, which, for those of you who haven't seen it, all I need to say is, Peter Sellers, Ringo Starr, *and* John Cleese. Now you are going to be starring in *The*

*Pink Panther 2*. Peter Sellers was associated with the Pink Panther movies, but *The Magic Christian* was a movie that you helped to write and you were also in, and so you have this sort of interesting cycle of the Peter Sellers connection in your very early career and again now, forty years or so later. I find that fascinating, and I wonder if you think that there is any sort of connection there that has meaning, given your interest in things that are mystical or psychological, or if it's just a coincidence.

CLEESE: No, I'm beginning more and more to think that there's something—I don't know what it is—what Carl Jung called "synchronicity." And I'm just convinced, the older I get, that this is kind of significant. I think that it is very strange that there I was on the exercise bicycle today and on comes Keith Olbermann, who is a sort of friend of mine but I haven't seen him in a while, and there he is with Bill Maher and they are talking about Cornell, and here I am sitting in Cornell. I don't know what it means, but there's something about it. I really believe that.

And I think that the more I read about quantum physics, the more I am quite convinced that this is a very much weirder universe than anyone knows. People get very *upset* with this kind of thing. If you want one example of what I am talking about, Google the following word: Gauquelin. This guy did statistical research that shows almost, I think incontrovertibly, that there is something—whatever it is, I don't know—to astrology. He shows that, for example, generals and athletes have Mars coming over the horizon at the time of their birth more than they statistically should, and artists and musicians have a lack of Mars influence in their charts. Now, you may think it's poppycock, but look at the statistics. It's very strange and yet no one is talking about this.

I had dinner last night with Daryl Bem, who shows—

MANNIX: He is a psychology professor here.

CLEESE: A really good guy. Great fun. He's also a magician. He's got a paper coming out that shows that there's such a thing as precognition, that people know in advance what's going to happen.

There's a guy, Dean Radin, who works in the Institute of Noetic Sciences, just north of San Francisco. He's done this experiment which has been reproduced in psychological departments at the best universities all over Europe. They put people in front of a television set and they then show them pictures. There are three types of pictures: there are neutral pictures, like a picture of a telephone or a parachute; there are sort of nice erotic, not very strongly erotic but slightly erotic, pictures; and then there are horrible pictures, which are pictures of accidents and operations, very bloody and nasty. And what they've shown is that if they put those pads that measure the galvanic skin response of people—you know, a measure of anxiety—what they have discovered is that before the nasty pictures, but *not* before the neutral pictures or the erotic ones, but before the nasty ones, which are being generated at random, there's a rise in the anxiety levels when people are about to see the nasty pictures. Now, how could they possibly know? They're not reacting in that way before they see a neutral image or when they see an erotic one. Two seconds beforehand, they know that they are going to see a nasty one. And the images are randomly generated. I think this is fascinating. But nobody takes it into account because it is contrary to the current paradigm.

But even if you forget all of that and just get into your own psychology, it is interesting that at fifteen, I saw this guy pouring water and claiming that there might have been a smoking cigarette butt and then, all this time later, here I am at Cornell having dinner with psychologists. There is a kind of shape.

And I think if you stay in touch with what you are really interested in, then your lives take on this kind of shape. But if you get pulled off center too much by thinking you have to earn lots of money and go for high status, then I think you can lose touch with your core. I mean, the question is, how much do you really need money to make you happy? All research shows not much. Right, Beta?

MANNIX: Yes, most of the research shows that there's very little cor-relation. I mean, after a certain sustenance level . . .

CLEESE: That's right. There's a certain level—and above that, more money doesn't make people happier.

MANNIX: [*To audience*] It's not going to make you happy. I know you all *think* it's going to make you happy, right?

CLEESE: People don't believe this—none of you believe this— but it's actually true. So if you can do what you are really deeply interested in, then I promise you, you'll have a pretty good life. And if you go on thinking that you have to do all sorts of things to gain other people's respect by getting high status and fame and a lot of money, I don't think you will have a particularly good life. But staying in touch with that core is the basis of it all. God, *I* can talk!

STUDENT: Hi. My name is Isaac Tates, and I'm a human development major, which is kind of a more holistic psychology. I'm really inter-ested in dream studies and, since you have such a marvelous mind, I wanted to know, what is your most vivid dreamworld? What is your dreamworld like?

CLEESE: I believe that dreams are incredibly important to some peo-ple. I don't think that they've been very important for me. Not to say that I'm not interested in them, but I think an awful lot of them are trivial. I think they're trivial because—there's been research done—if you are sleeping in a room that is very hot, you're going to have more of a certain type of dream, so in a sense, your dream's being dictated by the physical surroundings.

Sometimes you have a dream which is of *extreme* importance which has got a mythical quality to it; I've read about these dreams, but I don't remember if I ever really had one myself. So I don't find that is important for me.

What I *do* find is that the more I rely on some kind of gut feeling, it's partly intuition, but I think a lot of it is processed experience—an experience that has been processed on a very deep level. The more I rely on that, the happier I am. I sometimes used to go along with things which I didn't feel good about because I felt that I ought to go along with it, or the fact that I didn't feel quite right about it wasn't sufficient reason enough not to go along with it. But now, when I get that feeling that I'm really uncomfortable about something, I take it much more seriously than I used to, and I think it works for me.

But dreams themselves don't matter so much or they haven't had an impact. They may one day. Thank you.

STUDENT: I'm Allie from the College of Arts and Sciences. I was wondering what you feel the future of the British monarchy will be when Queen Elizabeth passes away.

CLEESE: Well, I'm profoundly apathetic about it. I don't really care either way. But I do think it's quite a good idea to split the head of state from the top political guy, and some countries do that with more or less a sort of a figurehead president, which I think it *is* an advantage.

But I've always been uninterested in the royal family because I think, with the basic exception of Charles, who *is* an interesting man, they're just not very interesting. They are tremendously keen on horseracing. There's nothing *wrong* with horseracing. I just don't think that people who are running countries should spend a lot of time watching horses run. It doesn't seem to me tremendously interesting, but that's a personal preference. They've always worked very well in England because they've never been tremendously interested in the arts, so they're not sort of *suspect* in Middle England. You see what I mean? The only one who was interested in the arts was Princess Margaret, and she was always by far the least popular of all the royals. So they were kind of middle-class people looked at as being very important. But I think that they have a useful symbolic function. But whether they're there or not, to me, is completely unimportant.

ALUMNUS: You know the quote, "There are three kinds of lies: lies, damned lies, and statistics." Do you know the original Milgram experiments? They were repeated last year and they found essentially the same result. What's your take on this?

CLEESE: Well, my take, I'm afraid, is that there are aspects of human nature which are not very attractive. Would you like to describe the Milgram experiments?

ALUMNUS: No, you can talk about them better than I can.

CLEESE: Because you've seen them more recently than I have. That was in one of the documentaries that I saw on television when I was fifteen that got me interested in psychology, but basically—

MANNIX: You mean the shock experiments?

ALUMNUS: Well, it was originally done to explain the Holocaust.

MANNIX: You mean the shock experiments in which people were told to shock someone in another room that they couldn't see, and to continue to shock them up to very, very high levels?

ALUMNUS: And after a while, they stopped screaming because they were presumably either unconscious or dead.

MANNIX: That's right.

ALUMNUS: They did it again last year, and the exact same results were found.

MANNIX: And the point was that they were instructed to do so by someone in a lab coat who was meant to be an authority figure.

ALUMNUS: Right. So that means that humans are not to blame?

MANNIX: That's why you accept the instructions.

CLEESE: I think humans hate being out of step. There's another experiment—I think it's Solomon Asch. This is what he did: He got some people together, and every single person in the room was a plant except for one. They put all the plants in a line, and they put that guy who *wasn't* a plant at the end of a row. Then they put up some lines on an easel and they asked which of the lines was longer: A or B? And it was absolutely clear that A was the longer line. So what happened, all the plants say: B, B, B, B, B, B. And they got to this guy on the end of the row and he didn't realize it was a setup. And he says A. They say, "Thank you. Thank you, very much."

Now they ask, which is the bigger circle: A or B? The plants all say: A, A, A, A, A, and it gets to him. Now, it's quite clear B is the bigger circle, so he says B. They say, "Thank you." There's no pressure on him. They just say, "Thank you, very interesting."

By the third time it goes down the line, he says the opposite of what he knows is the truth because he doesn't like disagreeing with all the other guys in the row. You see how tragic that is? There's no pressure on him. Nobody is being unpleasant. It's not like Nazi Germany where you could get beaten up if you said the truth. You see what I'm saying? And yet, the third time they went down the line, he was in agreement. So those are the things we really need to know about because it makes us very skeptical about how much can be achieved. We need to know about these things.

STUDENT: Thank you for coming, Mr. Cleese. You spoke earlier about creativity and its absence in the education system. Could you make a few recommendations on how we, as students at Cornell, could maybe pursue this aspect on our own?

CLEESE: Well, there is a book that I think is tremendously helpful and the book is called *Hare Brain, Tortoise Mind,* and that's h-a-r-e. *Hare Brain, Tortoise Mind* is by a guy called Guy Claxton, and I think it's wonderful. The next time I come to Cornell, I should do an explanation of it because what I say is different from what most people say, but I can give it to you in two minutes.

What it's really about is getting away from the everyday mode of thinking because, if we are under pressure, we tend to come up with stereotypical thoughts. And that's fine because, a lot of the time, we don't need to make complicated decisions. You know what I mean? If we're driving, we don't want to examine the situation; we just want to go and simply get it over with.

So a lot of stereotypical thinking is very, very useful, particularly if we are under time constraints because we can't examine everything, you know. As somebody once said, when you are attacking a machine gun nest, that is *not* the moment to admire the scenery. Or to have a breakthrough idea. Or see the funny side of it. Do you see what I mean? But when you want to be creative, you want to get away from the pressures that force you into stereotypical thinking.

And the way you do that is you need to create a space where you can play. There's a great book about play, and what I learned from it is that play has to be separate from ordinary life. In ordinary life, there is so much going on we have to remember and get done. You know what I'm talking about . . . this and that and that. Oh, I forgot that! It's very hard to be playful when you're carrying on and you've got other things on your mind and other things to get done.

You have to create a space, and you do that by creating boundaries of space and boundaries of time. You need space to avoid interruption. If you are a fat cat, you can sit in the office and say to your assistant, "Don't interrupt me for an hour and a half unless the building is burning down." If you are at the bottom of the hierarchy and you're young, then you may have to sit at a park.

I had a friend at Cambridge who came from a working-class family. He had four brothers and sisters and it was a tiny little house. The only place he could get any peace or space was to go into the toilet and sit there. That's where he studied for his Cambridge entrance exams.

You could sit in the park. You see, you have to get where there aren't any interruptions. That's the first thing. And the second thing is you give yourself boundaries of time. It starts at *this* moment and it stops at *that* moment. It's a little bit like a football (soccer) game: boundaries of space and there has to be a pitch, and the only people that are allowed on the pitch are the players. It starts when the referee blows the whistle and finishes when the referee says so. That's play. If you can become playful, that's how you become creative. And it's unrelated to intelligence, except that you have to be in the 95th percentile! So that's the key to it. It's creating a space where you can be playful.

AUDIENCE MEMBER: I'm not a student. My buddy said, "John Cleese is coming to Cornell." And I said, "Then I'm coming!" I mostly came because Monty Python and your work have been so influential for me—especially the humor because I'm not very funny at all. And you touched on it. Maybe you can talk a little bit more about humor. And I know it's probably a lot about psychology and the human mind for you, but I wonder whether you could talk about its function in teaching and society and how it can be used and all that sort of thing.

CLEESE: Okay, well I just did thirty-four hours in two seminars in San Francisco on this, so I'll try to boil it down a bit. I think the key is this: in any room where there is freedom, people are relaxed, people are content, they're not frightened, they're not anxious—in that room, there's going to be a feeling of ease and spontaneity. And so, there's going to be humor present because you can't be relaxed and spontaneous without there being some humor. There may be a lot, there may be less day by day. So, it's a kind of measure of, are people relaxed?

Now, that's a little bit different from jokes. I have a friend who traveled on a bus once and in the front were a lot of marines and everyone was telling jokes. He said what was interesting about it was that one would tell the joke and everyone would go sort of, "Ha ha ha ha ha har. Ha ha ha ha har." It was like a ritual. And what he noticed was there was no spontaneity. It was almost like a military exercise. Ha ha ha ha ha har.

When humor's around, there's a kind of intimacy because people are reacting and it becomes playful; it becomes fun. So I think when there's genuine humor, as opposed to just jokes, I think what happens is that people are relaxed, and that's very good creatively.

You know, I once interviewed the Dalai Lama.

MANNIX: I didn't know that.

CLEESE: Yes, and I said to him, "Why is it that Tibetan Buddhists are always in good spirits?" And he actually answered a slightly different question. He said, "What I like about laughter is that, when people laugh, they can have new thoughts." In other words, it's a kind of touchstone: when people are laughing, they are comfortable; where there's humor, a little bit of play, a little bit of gentle friendly teasing—if all of this is going on—it loosens up the mind.

Because if you just want people to go on having the same thoughts, put them under pressure. And that's why I think being around Cheney must be so awful. He knows everything. I mean, there's no real discussion there. He knows everything. And there's a sort of a feeling of anxiety around him. There isn't sort of an easy flow.

I have a feeling in the Obama meetings, there will be a little bit of humor there because there's sort of a flow about what is going on.

But there is a very interesting academic theory by a philosopher called Bergson, Henri Bergson, I think about 1890, 1900.

MANNIX: That's the time frame.

CLEESE: He wrote a book called *Laughter*, and he said something fascinating, which I really think this is good. He said, first of all, that it requires a momentary anesthesia of the heart because if you're watching something and it makes you laugh—think about Basil Fawlty—the moment you laugh ever so slightly, you withdraw some sympathy or empathy for the character. Otherwise, you couldn't laugh. You see what I mean? But that doesn't mean that it's cruel, because we can laugh at ourselves. It just seems for a moment we step back and see ourselves with a little bit of distance, and that's necessary before we can laugh. We have to have that slight distance because all humor is ever so slightly critical.

What Bergson goes on to say is that it's a social sanction because we laugh *together* as a group in society, and it's a sanction because we're trying to get people to behave flexibly. He said, what is invariably funny is when we start behaving like machines. That's why anyone, for example, who has an obsession is funny—because it is mechanical. They're not flexible anymore; they're obsessed with or by something. So all manifestations of human behavior that are fundamentally *not* flexible, Bergson says, we laugh at because, at a deep level, we want people to get more flexible. And I think that's very interesting.

The only trouble about humor is that I've always thought it depends on mental health; on one hand, you've got nasty humor.

You've got the nastiest kind of racial humor. It's unkind. It's punishing. It's not really very funny. It's a way of taking it out on a particular person or a particular group. And on the other hand, you've got the healthiest form of humor, which is basically saying, "Isn't this state that we are in as human beings absolutely extraordinary? Isn't it insane?" Because we are bound to biological principles—we're bound to that—and yet we can look at the stars. Oscar Wilde said, "I may be sliding into the gutter, but at least I'm looking at the stars." And here we are, in this extraordinary position of being held back by our ego and our bodily irritations, and yet we can do almost anything with our minds. And when we share that kind of humor—"Isn't it ridiculous?"—that's the best kind of humor because we're all in the same boat. It's absolutely opposite from the punishing kind of humor.

MANNIX: That was pretty extraordinary. I think we'll take one more question.

STUDENT: My name is Kevin, and I recently graduated as a creative writer and so, speaking to you as a writer, I was wondering have you ever created a character who was completely psychologically different from you, that you had to play? And did you enjoy playing someone who was radically different from yourself?

CLEESE: Well, the first character that comes to mind is a character I *didn't* play in *A Fish Called Wanda,* which was Kevin's character, Otto. And I have to tell you why I got the idea for the character, and I hope to God there isn't one of him out there. I was wondering what Kevin's character should be like, and I had a copy of *Los Angeles* magazine that I was leafing through, and there was this double-page spread advertising a seminar that was being given by this little man who was trying to look impressive but kind of looked a bit . . . well . . . he called himself Zen Buddhist Master Rama, and he had that hair like a full dandelion puff. I thought, "This guy does not look very impressive." And then I saw the headline, and I promise you this is what it said: "Buddhism gives you the competitive edge." I thought it was the *key* to Kevin's character. It was just a matter of writing. This is a man who has read everything and *understood* nothing.

So I started writing that, and when I started working with Kevin on the character, I more or less handed it over to him, and at times he would just improvise. For example, do you remember the smelling under the arm? He suddenly did that in the middle of an improvisation, and at the end of it, I said, "That was wonderful! What was that guy smelling under his arm?" He said, "What?" He was so deeply into the character that he hadn't even realized what he had done. He said, "Oh yeah, yeah, I did do that." I said, "Well, that's wonderful."

So then, as a writer you'll understand this: we introduced that on page thirteen and we repeated it on twenty-two, then we let the audience forget it and we did it again on page thirty-seven. Then we gave the audience a break and did it again on page sixty-four. You see what I mean?

That was a character that I enjoyed writing very much because he was so absolutely different. But there are other characters. For example, the *Fawlty Towers* guy was based on a fellow we actually met; the Pythons stayed at this man's hotel. He was so *gloriously* rude. The overriding principle he had was, I could run this place properly if it weren't for the guests.

# A CONVERSATION WITH JOHN CLEESE

## JOHN CLEESE AND DEAN JOHN SMITH,
Director, Cornell University Press

SEPTEMBER 11, 2017

PROVOST MICHAEL KOTLIKOFF: Good evening, everyone. I'm Michael Kotlikoff, Cornell's provost, and I have the pleasure *not* of introducing John Cleese, who hardly needs my introduction to this audience, but of telling you a little about his long association with Cornell University.

In 1999, Cornell first enticed John to come here as one of our A. D. White Professors-at-Large, intellectuals from around the globe who make periodic visits to Cornell to enliven our intellectual and cultural life. At that time, many people, of course, were admirers of his work on TV, his writing and acting in *Monty Python's Flying Circus*, his writing and starring with Connie Booth in *Fawlty Towers*, and in films like *Monty Python and the Holy Grail*, *Monty Python's Life of Brian*, and *A Fish Called Wanda*, which he wrote and for which he received a nomination for an Academy Award.

Since that time, John has been engaging, delighting, and stimulating Cornell students and faculty, as well as area fans. Discussing his films, as he did yesterday, conducting master classes for students and actors, leading discussions of group dynamics with film majors, and lecturing about creativity, John has consistently fascinated

Cornell audiences with his eclectic talks and performances that have demonstrated, along with his ingenious comic talent, his keen intellectual explorations into multiple fields. A few examples: he has given a sermon at Sage Chapel, narrated Prokofiev's *Peter and the Wolf* with the Cornell Chamber Orchestra, conducted a class on script writing, discussed religion in the Monty Python film *Life of Brian*, and lectured on psychology and human development.

Of course, John Cleese, all along, has continued to create, perform, and entertain: playing the role of Nearly Headless Nick in two of the Harry Potter movies, performing as the voice in numerous animated films, including *Charlotte's Web* and *Winnie the Pooh*, hosting a television special about football (aka soccer), and a BBC documentary about lemurs in Madagascar, and contributing to lemur conservation efforts, which led scientists to name a newly discovered species *Avahi cleesei* (Cleese's woolly lemur).

John's visits to our campus have been received with so much enthusiasm that Cornell took the unusual step of extending his six-year appointment as professor-at-large for another two years and, then, even after that, we couldn't let him go and cooked up another title: provost's visiting professor.

Please welcome the incomparable John Cleese.

DEAN SMITH: There's a dead bishop on the landing.

JOHN CLEESE: A dead bishop on the landing? What's its diocese?

SMITH: Haven't got a clue.

CLEESE: Well, it's tattooed on the back of its neck.

At lunchtime, Dean surprised me with that line, which I hadn't remembered for thirty years. We both laughed and I thought it was a good starting point today because sometimes very, very silly things have the ability to affect us deeply. Like,

A grasshopper hops into a bar.
The barman sees him.
The grasshopper hops onto the stool.
The barman says, "Oh, we've got a drink named after you."
And the grasshopper says, "What, Norman?"

This is sort of a silly joke you laugh at, and then you laugh at it again. I love that. It's like in *Life of Brian* when he starts saying,

"You've all got to think as individuals."
And they all say, "Yes, we've all got to think as individuals."
And Brian says, "You are all individuals."
They say, "Yes, we are all individuals."
And then one man says, "I'm not."

It doesn't mean anything, but it just makes you go on laughing, and I love that kind of thing. You don't get that with more clever or cerebral jokes, you know. You just get it with silly ones like bishops with their diocese tattooed on the back of their neck.

So, what are we going to talk about?

SMITH: Well, the pantomime elephant in the room really is Monty Python.

CLEESE: Monty Python, yes. It's funny how it's more loved here in the United States than it is anywhere else. If I go, for example, to Scandinavia or Australia or Britain, they're all on about *Fawlty Towers*. But here, Monty Python made a deep impression. It touched people at a very deep level. Many Americans have come up to me and said, "You got me through my exams at college." Friday nights they used to sit down and have a good laugh and decide that life was worth living after all.

It's very touching because there's no way we knew this would happen. When we were sitting in a room reading out things that we'd written in the previous week and we started to laugh, it was the first sign that we thought maybe it was funny. Just before we recorded the very first show, which started with a sketch about a sheep that was trying to teach the other sheep to fly because they knew what their ultimate fate was, Michael Palin and I were standing in the wings, and I said to Michael just before Graham Chapman and Terry Jones started the sketch, "You know, Michael, this could be the first time in history where people have recorded an entire comedy show to complete silence." And Michael said, "I was having the same thought." It felt that dangerous to us.

SMITH: Was there a moment when you knew you had something?

CLEESE: Yes, when that sketch went on, Michael and I were listening to it and suddenly there was a giggle, and then a bigger giggle, and then something approaching a laugh, and then there was a real laugh. And I remember thinking, "I think we're going to be all right!"

That's how little you know about what's going to happen to your work. How certain lines will—what do you say these days— "go viral." Certain lines become famous, and other lines that you love, no one ever notices or repeats.

SMITH: Like, "Pining for the fiords."

CLEESE: "Pining for the fiords." Everybody remembers that, but not the chocolate box sketch, when the health inspector goes to the Whizzo Chocolate Factory. He asks about these disgusting chocolates, and eventually he picks a chocolate out of the box and he says, "What is this one, Spring Surprise?" And the proprietor says, "When you bite into the chocolate, two sharp springs spring out and lacerate your cheeks." And the health inspector says, "Where's the pleasure in that?"

I always thought that was a really funny line. I want to say it to mountaineers, "Where is the pleasure in that?" But no one else ever picked up on that line.

Whereas the silly walk, which I never thought was particularly funny, it never really appealed to me, yet, everyone remembers that. At my age, at seventy-eight, they still say, "Will you do your silly walk?"

SMITH: It's the one where both legs fly out backwards.

CLEESE: Well, I now have a totally artificial knee and two artificial hips, so I can do a geriatric version of it, but it hardly involves any movement.

SMITH: So, talk about why, in America, *The Holy Grail* is more popular than *Life of Brian*.

CLEESE: Yes, that's very strange because in England there's no question they like *Life of Brian* better. But here it's always been *Holy Grail*.

There was a BBC poll about two weeks ago. They asked an enormous number of good, well-established critics from a lot of countries to list their favorite movies. Number one is still *Some Like It Hot*, which is really interesting because it's sixty years old. It's a great movie. Number four is *Groundhog Day*, which is one of my favorites and I'm seeing the musical on Sunday, which I'm really looking forward to. We had *Life of Brian* at number six and *Holy Grail* at number fifteen, which is not bad, you know. And then, further down the list, not that I take these polls too seriously, there's a fellow called Charlie Chaplin.

SMITH: So, today I read that *The Holy Grail* is one of the most authentically shot movies about the Arthurian legend.

CLEESE: Really?

SMITH: Yeah. Not peer reviewed.

CLEESE: Well, it probably was because Terry Jones knew a lot about medieval literature and quite a lot about medieval history.

But something like the coconuts . . . well, they say necessity is the mother of invention. All that stuff with those coconuts was genius, and that was Michael Palin's. When Michael read that sketch out to us, we said, "Well, what do you mean, the coconuts?" And he said, "Well, they've each got a page who claps them together like this." And we said, "How do they go along?" And he said, "Well, they go along like this," and he mimed their riding movements.

And we would never have thought of that if we'd had enough money for horses.

So that is what really got the creative juices going, and once we wrote that sketch, we began to see what the whole film was about. Because—you won't believe this—of the first draft, we threw out 90 percent. We had no idea what we were doing; we'd never done a movie before. But we staggered towards something that had some very, very, very funny sketches in it, which became scenes as we found ways of linking them together. But it still doesn't really have a story or a plot, and I think *Life of Brian* is better because it does have quite a good story.

SMITH: Absolutely.

CLEESE: It's why I prefer it.

SMITH: Some of the biblical study was first-rate.

CLEESE: You won't believe this, but this story is absolutely true. Three years ago, we did the Python show at the O2, which is this huge arena, sixteen thousand people. At the same time, in one of the London University colleges, King's College, they had a whole weekend of a proper academic conference about the effect that *Life of Brian* had on the study of Christian theology. They took it absolutely seriously, yes, there's a book out there on the conference. What was extraordinary to me was they felt that some of the jokes threw light on Christian teaching in a way that was original. It's astounding, but that's actually what they told me. They felt that we brought things up in the film that highlighted certain important subjects which hadn't been discussed before.

    You see, people can very easily get caught up in a traditional way of thinking. When I talk about creativity, it's really trying to get out of one's normal habits of thought. I remember saying to a senior theological lecturer, "It seems to me that when you read the beatitudes, the 'Blessed are the . . .' ones, they are all about trying to reduce the power of the ego." Which was, to me, so obvious. And he said, "I've never thought of that." Seriously. So sometimes, in comedy, we're not hampered by too much knowledge, so we can come up with stuff that does make people think.

SMITH: So, do you want to take a couple of audience questions?

CLEESE: Yes, sure.

SMITH: This is an anonymous question: "What was the most controversial Monty Python sketch you were part of?"

CLEESE: Oh, I think the undertaker sketch. Do you remember that? I do love that. It was very, very naughty. It was the last show of the third series, and Graham Chapman and I had been writing the show at that point for four years or something, and I said to Graham: "This is the last show we're going to do for a bit and I'm bored." And, he said, "So am I." And I said, "What are we going to write about?" He said, "Let's do something really naughty." So, I said, "Like what?" And Graham was a qualified doctor by that point. He said, "Something about dead bodies." So I said, "Right."

I'll tell you the sketch because it's wonderfully outrageous. I come in and I say, "I need your help because, well, quite simply, my mother's just died."

He says, "Oh, well, we deal with stiffs."

And that never gets a laugh, but it's funny.

And then he says, "Well, basically, there are three things we can do: we can bury her, we can burn her, or we can dump her."

And I say, "Dump her? What do you mean 'dump her'?"

He says, "Dump her in the Thames."

"Dump her in Thames!!!"

He says, "Well, did you like her?"

"Well, yeah."

"So we won't dump her in the Thames. So there's two things: we can burn her or bury her."

"Well, which do you recommend?"

He says, "Well, I'm not sure, really. If you burn her, you know, we shove her in the flames. Crackle, crackle, crackle. Which is a bit of a shock if she's not quite dead. But quick!

"Or . . . we put her in the ground and weevils and little maggots eat her up slowly. Which again," he says, "is not nice if she's not quite dead."

"Oh, she's definitely dead."

And then he says to me, "Where is she?"

And I say, "Oh, she's here in this sack."

I pull the sack around.

He looks inside and says, "Oh, she was quite young."

"Yes, yes."

He says, "Fred, I think we've got an eater."

There was a gasp from the audience. I love that intake of breath. They're thinking, "What's he going to say next?"

I say, "What? What? You're not suggesting . . . *eating* . . . my mother."

And he says, "Well, not raw, you know. Cooked."

I think it's wonderful. A lot of the audience thinks it's hilarious, right? And then I look at them, and there are some people sitting there with their heads in their hands.

SMITH: Yeah, I didn't know if you were going to go all the way with that one.

CLEESE: I can't even remember how it finished on the television. They allowed us to do it, which was great, on the condition that the studio audience invaded the set in protest. But when Eric and I do it on tour, it's just wonderful how it makes people laugh. When you're talking about eating your dead mother, you can't get much naughtier than that. That was the naughtiest.

SMITH: This question is similar, by Jeffrey Tokman: "What is your favorite Monty Python sketch to watch?"

CLEESE: To watch? Oh, it might surprise you. It's in *The Holy Grail* and it's a scene with Michael and Eric and Graham Chapman. There are two guards, and Michael is trying to tell the guards, "Just keep my son in this room." It's so wonderfully performed. Eric and I show this clip every night, and it still makes me laugh that the guards just don't get it. There's something terribly funny about stupidity, you know. Provided you're not on the receiving end of it.

Well, sometimes when you're on the receiving end, it is quite funny. About six months ago, I was in Miami. I shouldn't be making Miami references, but it did happen to be in Miami. I had a massage in the spa, and afterwards I went up to my room and I got a phone call saying, "Mr. Cleese, you left your slippers in the spa. Can we send them up?" So, I say, "Yes, of course. Thank you very much."

Three minutes later: *knock, knock.* I go to the door and the man says, "Mr. Cleese, here are your slippers." He gives them to me in a bag and I say, "Thank you very much."

And he says, "Could I have some identification?"

So I said, "Well, you know my name, right, because you just called me Mr. Cleese. And . . . you know my room number."

He said, "But could I have some formal identification?"

So I remembered that I had a copy of my autobiography with me. I got my autobiography and I went back to the door and held it up right next to my face and pointed to and fro. "That's the name, you see, that's my name, you see, I'm John Cleese. That's the same person."

And he looked at me and he said, "I'm afraid that's not good enough."

Isn't that wonderful? There's something about pure stupidity.

SMITH: So, we were talking yesterday about movies, and especially today's comedies. They don't tend to stick in my mind the way classic comedies do. They stand the test of time.

CLEESE: When I say to people now, "What was the last really classy comedy you saw?" there's usually a complete silence while they try to think of one because Judd Apatow has cornered a particular kind which, I think, is summed up in *Hangover*. The problem with *Hangover* is it's funny, but it's about drugs, gambling, sex, alcohol, celebrity—that's a very limited palette with which to paint the comic picture. Do you see what I mean?

I always wanted to do a film about 1776 because there's so much about it that's funny, which all gets covered up by the myths, you know. Basically, a third of the Americans were pro-British, a third of them were anti-British, and a third really didn't give a damn. That, itself, is quite funny. Another thing that always made me laugh was that most of the British troops were actually German. They were from Brunswick and Hesse and Hannover, and I thought if you started the movie with the British troops saying, "Ja, das ist der Führer (German-sounding gibberish)." Then you cut to the American trenches and they say, "Goddamn British."

And everyone in the film world told me, "John, they won't know enough about it."

The audience here tonight would, but that is very rare now. You see, it's young men who go to the cinema, and most other people don't, so the studios make movies for them. So you wind up with *Hangover* because that's their frame of reference: women and drugs and sex and alcohol and gambling. I think it means the movies become not very interesting anymore. You see, it boils down to economics and the fact that more and more grownups are not going to the cinema.

You know, I was in a couple of Bond movies, which I loved. I really enjoyed it. I got on well with the producers. They used to let me fiddle with the dialogue in my own scenes, and it was a thoroughly good experience. I loved working with Pierce Brosnan. He is a lovely man, totally professional, gets everything right, no fuss at all—all done in a nice, friendly low-key spirit. Incidentally, I only did four days of filming spread over four years. Not a big contribution, you know. It didn't dominate my life.

But what happened was that the studio discovered it was making huge amounts of money in the Far East: China, South Korea, the Philippines. And, of course, those audiences didn't understand the nuances of the jokes about British society or the class system or anything like that. What they loved were the action sequences. So, slowly, the studio realized there was a vast Asian audience to lure to the cinema, and the audience in Britain who *were* getting the little jokes was so tiny that they just gave up the jokes, and it all became about long action sequences. Action sequences should be something like three minutes of really intense action; then you really feel it. If they start lasting for fourteen minutes, it's too long, right? Studio people are always going where the money is, and that ultimately spoils most things.

SMITH: Now, what's happening in 2019 for Monty Python? There must be a big fiftieth-anniversary celebration.

CLEESE: Oh, yes, the Victoria and Albert Museum is having what they call a "retrospective," similar to the ones on David Bowie and Pink Floyd. It's everything we can find: costumes, scripts, props, reviews, all this kind of thing. It's going to last for six months and then going on tour in places like Tokyo and Paris and Berlin. So it's rather fun. I'm quite looking forward to that because we're all much too old and doddery to perform anymore.

Although the last Monty Python show, in 2014 at the O2 Arena, was a huge success. And it taught me something about comedy which I'd not realized before. You see, I always thought it was jolly good to make people laugh. And, of course, it's nice doing it. You enjoy making people laugh; it feels good. But I always thought of it as just entertainment.

One night when I was doing the Pepperpot sketch with Terry Jones, I had about ten seconds before they put the spotlights on us, and I was able to look out into the audience and see sixteen thousand people and, you know, they were all having a really good time. Of course, it wasn't an ordinary comedy show because the audience knew the lines better than we did. That's very unusual, even Shakespearean scholars don't go to *Hamlet* and know every single line. And I realized it wasn't a stage show; it was some kind of happening or event or occasion. We were making them laugh. And they were thanking us for having made them laugh, and we were thanking them for thanking us, and it was a celebration. People were very happy. There's not as much of that around these days.

A few days later, I was on a TV chat show with Neil Diamond, and he started to sing "Sweet Caroline" and all the audience stood up and, suddenly, I had the same feeling. There were lots of people gathered together, and there was a good spirit in the room. Everybody was friendly, happy, and having a good time. I suddenly thought: this is really important.

SMITH: Absolutely.

CLEESE: Because there's so much less of that these days with everyone focused on problems.

SMITH: Another question from Stephanie Heslop: "Describe the worst first date you've ever been on."

CLEESE: I can't; they were all pretty terrible. Well, they used to be. I was so hopeless, as we used to say, with women. Is that a sexist thing to say?

SMITH: No.

CLEESE: You have to be so careful these days.

I was hopeless with young women because there was so much I didn't understand. You see, I'd had a very uneasy relationship with my mother. Emotionally, it was not a good relationship. She was a very neurotic woman, very neurotic. She is the only person I've ever met in my life who used to write her worries down so that she wouldn't forget any of them. She had this vast spectrum of anxiety, you see. And she thought that if she spent enough time worrying about them all, she'd somehow manage to keep them at bay by the actual *act* of worrying. She kept the bad things at bay, and she seemed to believe if she forgot to worry about one of them, it would come and get her.

I tell you, if you have a mother like that, it takes some time to get better. Which is why I've spent about a quarter of my life in psychiatrist chairs and another quarter in dentist chairs—because I'm a war baby. I have the worst teeth in the world.

I'm rambling, aren't I? It's because I'm very, very old.

SMITH: There was some line in your book about your father and you walking on eggshells.

CLEESE: That's right, yes. Well, she did have a pretty mean temper. I always say there was only one thing that my mother wanted, just *one* thing—that was her own way. And if she didn't get it, there was trouble. There were tantrums and a great deal of noise, and Dad, who'd fought in the First World War for three and a half years, I think, sometimes yearned for the relative tranquility of the trenches.

SMITH: There was another scene where you've come back to visit your parents, and you suggest taking them to the movies.

CLEESE: Oh, yes, that's right. Don't forget that old people, even as old as I am, become anxious about all the things that can potentially happen. I would come down to Weston-super-Mare to spend three or four days with them and it was hard work. One day I said, "How about going to the movies this afternoon?" And this alarmed them. "What, well, what?" Mother would say, "But we going to go before tea or after tea?" Dad would go to the window and start looking at the weather. It's as if I'd said, "Why don't we invade Poland?" In the end, I'd say, "Well, let's not go to the movies," because it was causing so much alarm and despondency.

I had a wonderful psychiatrist once. Not only was he Viennese and Jewish but he knew Freud—he'd actually met Freud. I was talking to him about a problem I was having and he said to me, "John, tell me—did things happen easily in your family?"

SMITH: How did you get on with your father?

CLEESE: I had a very nice relationship with Dad. I loved him very much and he was very kind. The fact I'm not psychologically scarred for life is entirely due to that dear man. Mum was very, very good at everything that had to do with providing the meals and making sure everything was clean and tidy . . . she was terribly good at that. It was just that emotionally she was lacking because she was so full of fear. For people who are always worrying about what's going to happen next, life is a series of hurdles. "God, we've got to eat breakfast this morning; how are we going to get through that?"

My mother had no energy left over for thinking about anything but survival. But she spoke impeccable English, never made grammatical mistakes when she spoke. She also wrote very good English. She didn't make spelling errors. She wasn't highly educated, but she was very literate. *But* she had no general knowledge at all because she was only interested in what was about to affect her life in the next few minutes. So anything more than about ten feet away from her wasn't relevant, you see.

The result was that she went through life without acquiring any factual information. So that once, for example, my ex-wife made a salad with very small quail eggs in it—I don't know if you've ever seen quail's eggs; they are tiny, tiny, completely pointless eggs—and my mother said, "Oh, these, what are these little eggs?" And I said, "Well, they're moles' eggs." And she said, "Really?" And I said, "Yes, you see, on Sunday mornings Alyce Faye goes up on Hampstead Heath because, when the moon is very bright, moles lay their eggs at the mouth of the burrow, you see." And she goes, "Really! I never knew that."

One time, she said she'd heard somebody talking about Mary, Queen of Scots. "Who is that? I've heard her name before. Who is Mary, Queen of Scots?" I said, "Well, she was a Scottish caber tosser who got killed during the Blitz." She said, "How sad!"

The extraordinary thing was she lived so long. She was born in 1899, and she lived to the year 2000.

SMITH: Wow.

CLEESE: Extraordinary because her life spanned the entire twentieth century. From the assassination of Archduke Ferdinand in Sarajevo, the First World War, the Great Depression, the rise of Hitler and Stalin, the Second World War, the atomic bomb, the Cold War, the space age, the collapse of Communism—she lived through it all. Without really noticing any of it.

SMITH: Let's talk about the present. So, this is the first time you've been back at Cornell in a while. What have you been up to?

CLEESE: Well, let me tell you the whole story. Back in 2000, some people at Cornell contacted me and I said, "What do you mean, a visiting professor? What am I supposed to do?" And they said, "Well, you have to come up here twice a year and stir things up a bit." It was such a wonderful invitation. So I had a great seven years, and then they extended it indefinitely. But two years after that I was hit by a ridiculous divorce bill and I had to find $20 million. Which is a lot, you know. You can't pay someone $20 million just by sitting around watching television. So I just worked and worked and worked and worked and worked. Finally, I cleared it all off and I'm fine now. I've got my head back above water, so now I hope to come back regularly again.

SMITH: So what are you working on now?

CLEESE: I'm writing a show which, in many ways, began in Cornell when I met David Dunning. Now, David's a stunning social psychologist who's always been fascinated by how good people were at knowing how good they were at doing things; in other words, self-assessment. He carried out a series of tests with a young student called Kruger, and what they discovered was that the skill set one needs in order to know how good you are at something requires almost exactly the same skill set as it does to be good at that thing in the first place. What a wonderful corollary! It explains so much of the world: if you are absolutely no good at something, you lack *exactly* the skills and aptitude which you need to know that you're no good at it.

It explains a great deal because what happens as you get older, and I promise you I'm not exaggerating, is that you begin to realize, first of all, that almost *nobody* knows what they're doing or what they're talking about. Very, very few. The great thing about being in Cornell is that there *are* a few people around who *really do* know about something. And that's very rare.

But I'd had another, similar epiphany. I wrote two books with the psychiatrist Robin Skynner, who was a remarkable guy. He was a bomber pilot during the war. You know, there are not many psychiatrists who were bomber pilots during the war. Hard to imagine Sigmund Freud as a Dambuster.

One day I asked him, "Robin, in your profession, how many people, what percentage of psychiatrists, really know what they're doing?" He said to me, "About 10 percent." And I was shocked. From then on, whenever I met someone who I just instinctively knew was particularly good at their job, I would say, "How many people in your profession really know what they are doing?" I never got an estimate higher than 20 percent. I asked the question many times. Sometimes it was as low as five. But it was normally 10 to 15 percent. That was most people's guess.

So that means six out of seven people don't *really* know what they're doing. They learn a process or a procedure, but if that doesn't work, then they're lost, like me when my computer crashes. Do you see what I mean? So this is quite a starting point if six out of seven people don't know what they're doing.

So I'm writing this show called *Why There Is No Hope*. And when I start out, I say to the audience, "You know, a lot of you have come here to hear me tell you why there is no hope, and you think I mean it humorously. But I don't." And I then point out to them why there is absolutely no hope. There's always been no hope, but it's even worse now.

Shall I tell you something interesting? I met a man—you will hardly believe this—in Sarajevo four weeks ago who runs one of the biggest, if not *the* very biggest, marketing companies in America. He told me how he has profiles of somewhere between 185 and 190 million people, of what this person likes and doesn't like. We were talking about attention span and he said, "Do you know, in 1990, when they measured the average attention span, for young people it was about fifteen seconds. Today, a millennial's attention span is now six seconds. Now, I want you to guess what the attention span of a goldfish is. It's nine seconds."

How can there be any hope in a society where people have less attention span than a goldfish? And when highly trained professionals mostly don't know what they are doing?

And I can go on and on and on and on. I had a minor problem with a little bit of surgery in my leg. I had to go and see a specialist at Cromwell Hospital. We started chatting and he said, "Do you know that during the doctors' strike in New York a few years ago, the death rate went down?" So I got on the computer and looked; there are some wonderful statistics there. There was a major analysis done of five different doctors' strikes by a very respected academic medical journal, and in no case did the death rate go up. In three out of five of the cases, it went down. When cardiologists leave the hospital and go to conferences, the death rates at the hospital drop. But the good news is when they come back from the conference, the death rate recovers.

Then, I was with my cardiologist a few weeks ago—well, when you're my age, you spend most of your time talking to doctors, really. I said to him, "What's this about sugars and fats?" He said, "John, for sixty years, we cardiologists have got it wrong. It's not fats that cause heart trouble; it's sugars." I said, "Wrong? For *sixty years?*" He said, "Yes." I said, "But what was wrong with the research?" He said, "Oh, well, it's much easier to get funding for research projects that confirm the current paradigm." Do you see what I mean? If you challenge the current paradigm, you don't get funds for doing that, so nobody challenges it.

You see, that's the sort of stuff we're up against. So that's why I say there is absolutely no hope. There's less hope at the moment, of course, due to President Trump. His presidency is the most extraordinary thing that's happened in my lifetime. I couldn't believe that people had voted for him. It reminded me, when I was eighteen, I went to professional wrestling for the first time at the Colston Hall, Bristol. These huge hulks came out, and they were wonderful athletes—wonderful, but terrible actors, just laughable, the worst acting you've ever seen in your life. And yet, the alarming thing was that about 40 percent of the audience thought it was real. Now, if they can't see with their own eyes that it's phony, how can you explain to them that it's phony? That's how I felt about people voting for Trump. Can't they see that he's hopeless?

Although Trump supporters have given me my biggest laugh. In 2016, when a woman was asked about that recording that was made when he talked with a young chap called Billy Bush—please excuse the bad language but do you remember what he said? What he said was, if you were a celebrity, then women more or less expected you to grab their pussies. Do you remember he said that? And a middle-aged woman, who was a Trump supporter defending him, was asked about his making that remark and she said, "Well, he would never have said that if he'd known he was being recorded."

But the great thing about realizing that things are completely hopeless is that you start to relax. Next, your aims become more realistic. You say, "I tell you what—instead of changing society, I'll just be nice to a dozen people instead." Because that's achievable. Do you see what I mean?

SMITH: So, Cynthia M. asks: "What is the secret to a happy life?"

CLEESE: Oh! Well, quite seriously, I think it's about having modest aims. The most important thing in life, apart from finding the right person to be with, is to find something, a job that you find interesting. What helps most here is to realize how much money you really need.

There's a wonderful statistic, which is something like 33 percent of the American population believe that they are going to be billionaires within the next five years. Many of them are going to be disappointed, aren't they? So don't glamorize money.

A close friend of mine was talking to a doorman at an extraordinarily expensive apartment block in New York where many of the residents are billionaires. And the doorman, who sees them going in and out every day, commented that they never seem to be happy.

In America, in particular, there's a sort of feeling that if you're not rich and famous, you're sort of a failure. You've missed the boat. And this is the most pernicious attitude because, for centuries, we had people who were quite content to be part of a community and to do a job well and to have good friends in the community and to bring up children. That was considered a good life, but now it's not good enough. Well, that means that 99.9 percent of the population is going to be disappointed. So the first thing is keep your aims achievable.

The second thing is don't have children. You're laughing, but children cause most of the misery in the world. If you have children, you worry yourself sick about them, they cost a fortune, and then they grow up like their mothers. So avoid children.

Instead, have cats. Yes, because cats are *fantastic*. They're absolutely wonderful; they're affectionate when they feel like it, and they're just a pleasure to have around. My wife and I have four cats—three of them are American, Maine coons. One of them is bigger than she is. It's the biggest cat I've ever seen in my life. She's having a saddle made so that she can ride it. And the nice thing about cats is when they grow up, they don't blame you for everything.

SMITH: Earlier we were talking about Cornell students and how hard they work.

CLEESE: Oh, yes!

SMITH: You could sum up what we were discussing—a message for them that you have.

CLEESE: I was telling Dean about the first observation I made when I started coming to Cornell. I remember being very impressed by the students, everywhere. They had a real pride in being at Cornell. They felt really good about it. And when I said, "Well, give me some criticisms," they had to think for a bit and they said, "They work us too hard, of course." I said, "Really?" "Oh, yes," they said, "the work is very hard."

So when I started chatting to some of the professors, I said, "The students think that you work them too hard." The professors said, "Well, we do." I thought this was very odd. I said, "Well, if they think you work them too hard, and you think so too, are we moving towards some sort of plan here?" And one professor said, "Well, maybe it's because we're not Harvard or Yale."

This sums up to me one of the greatest problems that we have in America, which is that I don't think many of us know how to live very well. There's such an emphasis on acquisition and money and fame and all this. When I was in Sarajevo—and this is not a very wealthy part of the world—they were all having a marvelous time, and I was very struck by this.

A doctor friend went sailing during a sabbatical year, and as he traveled down the coast of South America, he would tie up the yacht and go inland. He said he'd never seen such poverty in his life, but everyone was happier than they were in America. Call me old-fashioned, but I think happiness is a jolly-good aim. As the Dalai Lama says, "Everyone wants to be happy." It's just we don't know how to go about it because our culture is sending us the wrong signals.

There are two things I would love to do for television. I would love to do a series of documentaries about what religion would be if the churches hadn't screwed it up. That would be fascinating. And the other thing is I would love to do a program about why very rich people want even more money. I think it's crazy. But the trouble is these very rich people own most of the newspapers and television stations, so these ideas don't get talked about much because it means challenging the belief systems of your employers.

Maybe it's a revolutionary idea, but I think people should do what they want. And yet people decide it's having a bigger car that will make them happier. There's a dominant credo of mindless competitiveness which doesn't really help anyone.

I grew up in England in the '50s and it was still strangely and, in some ways rather nicely, old-fashioned. And the dominant ideas were not about becoming very rich. During the whole time I was at Cambridge, between 1960 and 1963, I only ever met one person who wanted to go into business. Money was not that important. It didn't mean there wasn't competitiveness. Lots of people wanted to go to the BBC and, if they went into the BBC, it mattered whether their carpet went to the walls of the room or whether it stopped a few feet from the edge. That determined where they were in the hierarchy. Those silly competitive things didn't go away, but there was none of this obsession about cash as a measure of your worth as a human.

You will hardly believe this, but when I started work in 1966 with David Frost in his show, I was paying income tax at the rate of 83 percent! So you'd go in and work, Monday to Friday. Your take-home pay was what you'd earn on Friday after 10:30 a.m.; the rest went to the taxman. We were used to that. In Scandinavia, you find the level of happiness is far, far higher than it is in America. For all the talk about what a great economy America has, the people in Scandinavia know they're going to be looked after healthwise, and so there isn't that burning anxiety of what happens if you get seriously sick. That's a terrible fear to be carrying around.

Yet people who've never been to any other country—in fact, if you mention the word *abroad* to them, they don't really know where that is—these people will fight for the American way. Trump supporters are angry that they don't have a better lifestyle but are resolutely determined not to consider socialism, when it's capitalism that's delivered them the sort of society that they live in. I must be careful. That was a very inflammatory thing to say.

SMITH: So, what course would you want to teach if you were here full time?

CLEESE: Oh, how interesting. Maybe I'd want to teach how to be happy. You know, twenty years ago there weren't any books about this issue; it's very strange. Now there are lots of books about happiness and positive attitudes, thank goodness. But writing these two books with Robin Skynner, thirty years ago, I realized that the odd thing about psychiatry was that it was all based on the study of people who weren't doing very well. If you were writing a book about how to play better golf, you wouldn't consult the worst players in the world. You'd go to the good ones. In fact, the extraordinary thing about Robyn Skinner was that he was one of the few psychiatrists I've ever met who was seriously interested in what constituted good mental health and what were the characteristics of people who had it.

But you asked, "What would I teach?" I'd try to teach something to do with psychology because I don't think there's anything more interesting than the human mind. This is stuff that affects our lives, you know, what I've been talking about this evening. It actually gives us ideas about how to *live* our lives. Whereas no matter how good the teaching, if you're studying geology, that's not going to help you when you get home.

SMITH: So, related to that, talk about what was one of the happier times in your life.

CLEESE: Well, I'm happier now than I've ever been. But I don't say that in England because it annoys the press. If the papers find out you say you are happy and have got a nice marriage, they can't wait to find out something to disprove it.

Most important, after many, many—sorry, multiple—attempts, I have married somebody who I just adore. She's totally lovable in a way that I've never come across before, and she loves me in a way I've not been loved before. It seems to have removed a kind of deep anxiety that I've had so much of my life because to me that relationship is more important than my work. And then, as I've already told you, we have four cats.

So if somebody now said to me, "If you work really hard on this part, you will earn an Oscar," I would say, "Well, how hard do I have to work?" Because I don't need an Oscar. For most entertainment people, that would be the high point of their life. It isn't. It's not what life is about. But my life is now about quite simple things. And right at the moment, I find extraordinary pleasure in looking at trees. You just sit and look at them and they make you feel good.

SMITH: We publish a lot of books on trees.

CLEESE: Well, I think trees should have a vote; they're only about three IQ points lower than Trump supporters anyway. Whoa, at this point in the show I do with Eric Idle, people start walking out.

SMITH: So . . . Priya Srikumar asks: "What are your top tips for seduction?"

CLEESE: Seduction? I'll be honest—for years I was embarrassed and uptight and totally English with women. And I think it was because of my relationship with my mother and going to a single-sex school. When I went to Cambridge, there were two hundred people studying law with me and three of them were women, so I just didn't know how to relate to them, and I think I thought, having been to the James Bond films, that there must be a sort of button that, if I pressed it in myself, I'd suddenly become masterful or effortlessly macho or something. Finally, I learned that if you can be yourself and not show off too much, then it's very easy to see whether a woman likes you or not. That's better than spending a long time pretending to be someone else. Because eventually they find out who you really are anyway, and you've wasted a lot of time.

The other thing, of course, is to pretend to be actually be interested in them! When I went to Australia for the first time, I started to become successful with girls because they couldn't get over the fact that I actually listened to what they said. You see, this was not part of the Australian culture, so it seemed to be a very powerful aphrodisiac. A bit like Northern Ireland, you know, when they used to go to dances and the men would be at one end of the hall and the women would be at the other, and occasionally they would dance against each other.

SMITH: So, we can move to psychology: how well do we know ourselves?

CLEESE: Not at all. I think the great problem is that we're basically run by our unconsciousness and very few people are really interested in digging a bit deeper to find out.

I had two friends in school—they're both now professors—one is in New Orleans and the other is at McMaster in Canada. One is basically a neurologist, the other's a psychologist. They've both been very successful in their lives, and I've stayed in touch with them all these years, and neither one of them has ever meditated. I find that extraordinary: a professor of psychology who has never sat quietly and observed his own mind. So that's what I think we're up against—that people aren't terribly interested in exploring themselves. An English psychiatrist once said to me, "John, most Englishmen know much better what's going on under the bonnet of a car than they do in their own minds."

One of the most interesting things said about Trump is that he's very, very uncomfortable with the idea of self-reflection. Tony Schwartz, the coauthor of *The Art of the Deal*, who spent more time alone with Trump than almost anyone else has—about eighteen months—said that if he was asked any questions about his own internal processes, he just was very uncomfortable. And Trump once admitted to Schwartz, "I don't want to find out about stuff like that because I might not like it."

I think a lot of people feel that they don't really want to find out what's going on in themselves because we all have good and bad in us. Mother Teresa took up her work when she realized one day that she potentially had a Hitler living within her. She saw that she had the capacity for evil, and she simply chose to do something about it. In my case, for example, I can sometimes tell when I become envious, which is a particularly English trait. And because I recognize the feeling as envy and can say to myself, "Oh, I'm becoming envious," that gives me control whether I act out of my envy. Do you see what I mean? If I didn't realize I was being envious, I'd think there was something bad about the person that I was envious of. I would start making negative remarks about them. But if you think, "Oh, I'm feeling envious," well then, that's all right, it's just a feeling. It doesn't mean you have to *do* anything about it, you see, you're just aware of the emotion.

SMITH: And the work you did on yourself, did that affect your work?

CLEESE: Yes, it did, and Robin Skynner told me, "A lot of artistic people are worried that, if they go into therapy and examine themselves, they'll lose their creativity." He didn't feel that was true at all, which helped me. I think, now, that I'm more creative but I'm less *driven*. A lot of people confuse the two. They think that somebody who's very productive is very creative. A lot of driven people are very, very, very productive but not very creative at all. Also, if you're driven, then you really ought to know what's driving you, you know. You really ought to try and work it out because, otherwise, what are you doing with your life? You're on automatic. Not very dignified.

SMITH: So do you find it any easier to be creative now?

CLEESE: Well, I know how to facilitate it now. It's all about creating a space. Space is exactly the right word. That means you have to create boundaries—of time and of space. So first, you have to find a place where you can just be quiet. If you've got an office with a secretary, you say to the secretary, "I don't want to be interrupted for an hour, unless the building is on fire." If you're very junior, you may have to sit in the park. I had a friend at Cambridge who came from a poor working-class family and, if he needed to be quiet at his house, he would go and sit in the loo and bolt the door and study in there because it was the only place where he could be alone. So you have to create boundaries to keep people from interrupting you, because interruptions are absolutely fatal to creativity. You have to be able to let your mind free. The moment the outside world comes in and interrupts you, you're not doing that anymore.

The second vital thing is you can't be creative unless you can play—and play has got to be separated from everyday life. So you've got to have a time boundary; trying to be creative starts here and ends there. If you create these boundaries, then you start getting in touch more and more with little notions and images that start floating around. They're only the *beginning* of proper ideas, but if you explore them gently, they may take shape. It's just like meditating. At the start, your mind's all over the place for a bit and then, as the Buddhists say, it's like cloudy water—it slowly settles and becomes clearer, and then you can begin to hear the little promptings, from your unconscious mind.

The interesting thing psychologists have found is that scientists often have their most important ideas when they're in a slightly dreamy state, you see, not when they're feeling all gung ho. Edison used to sit in a very comfortable leather armchair, and he used to have a little metal tray, and he used to have ball bearings in his hand because he liked to be at that little twilight area between being asleep and awake. So he'd sit there, and if he dozed, his hand would relax and the ball bearings would drop into the metal tray and wake him up, and he would pick them up and start again. Also, the guy who discovered the structure of the carbon ring, August Kekulé, was very tired late one night and as he was sitting, watching the flames in the fireplace, he suddenly got the idea that they were snakes and they were chasing their own tails. That's how he realized that the carbon molecule was a ring.

So, when these greatest of all scientists make their discoveries when they're in this very dreamy state, it's *completely* the opposite of what we're taught about needing to think decisively. The research shows that one of the characteristics of creative people is that they defer decisions much longer than most people do, because they can tolerate that vague feeling of irritation and uncertainty that you get if you haven't resolved something. Some people just can't tolerate that. They've *got* to resolve an issue, so they take the decision before they actually need to take it.

I had this company that made management training films and the most important thing that I ever learned is, if you have a decision to take, the first question is, when does this decision have to be made? Because that's the real world—it's got to be taken before this or that happens. Well, okay, but *don't* make the decision before then. So if you're going to be creative, you must tolerate the uncertainty, because two things can happen. First of all, you may get new information which would affect the decision, and I experience that a lot. People want decisions and I say, "I'm not sure yet. I'm not sure yet." And then, during the course of the week, it just becomes obvious. So find out when the decision has to be taken and try to defer it until then, because secondly, it also gives your mind more time to come up with new ideas.

Everything I'm saying to you, instinctively, you know it's right. You just think it's unusual because we're not taught this at school, but it feels right. I mean, who at school ever said to you what I'm saying to you now? It should be a basic part of education, and yet nobody teaches it. It's quite crazy.

Am I going on a bit?

SMITH: Well, no. I have a question, though, from the audience.

CLEESE: We should probably tell them a joke.

Why do the French have so many civil wars?

So that they can win one now and then.

SMITH: From Dan Zimmerman: "What's your favorite *Fawlty Towers* moment?"

CLEESE: I'll tell you exactly. It's when Basil runs down to the town to get the duck and he gets a strawberry mousse by mistake. My favorite moment is, he brings it back and the diners have been waiting for their duck for an hour, and he puts it down and lifts the top off and sees the strawberry mousse and he immediately replaces the lid, as though, somehow, he's buying himself time. And then he lifts the top again and feels inside the strawberry mousse in case there's a duck in there.

SMITH: So, you travel the world visiting corporations and talking to executives. What are some of the things going on when you do that?

CLEESE: Well, I'm always a bit suspicious about some corporations. I think there are a lot of people in the food industry and in the pharmacy industry who are not really interested in helping people to lead healthier lives. They'd rather hush up any research that shows that the thing they're selling is harmful. And that's wicked. But, in my own experience working with executives, I've always been surprised at how decent they are. They really love to make things work, and they love to create an organization where people feel that they belong and where they can do good work and, you know, just generally contribute something. So, because I do think rigid, bottom-line thinking is at the heart of so much that's not right with America, I'm confused about it.

SMITH: What are the traits of the most successful leaders that you've seen?

CLEESE: They're lucky! Napoleon said, "Don't give me good generals; give me lucky ones."

SMITH: Okay, let's talk a little bit about spirituality and religion, and how has that evolved—your spiritual journey over time?

CLEESE: Well, I was Church of England, which was once described as "the Conservative Party at prayer." When I took confirmation classes, nothing interesting was ever discussed, and after I was confirmed—I was fifteen—I waited for about four weeks for some golden haze to come down and boost me spiritually. When nothing happened, I just gave up and decided it was complete rubbish.

Much later, in my thirties, I started reading books by an Englishman who came to California, called Alan Watts, and I started learning stuff about Eastern religion, which began to make some sense to me. Then I had a breakthrough. I read a chapter in a book called *The Human Situation*, by Aldous Huxley, in which he basically says there are two types of religion: There is the more meditational type, where people are actually interested in seeing whether they can have some sort of experience of the divine. And these people do spiritual exercises. If they're Sufis, they dance. If they're Jewish, they're interested in the Kabbalah. If they're interested in Christianity, they study esoteric Christianity. These are the people who believe there is something out there that they can connect with if they are prepared to spend a lot of time in spiritual practices, to find out more about themselves and trying to have an experience of the divine. That's one type of religion.

And then there's the other type of religion, which is basically crowd control. There is the great headmaster in the sky; here are the rules—stick to the rules and you'll go to heaven and you'll be able to eat all the ice cream you want without getting fat.

But what I've realized is so astonishing, that people can take a religious teaching and turn it on its head. Pope Pius X, in 1906, said, "Kindness is for fools." You'd think, since he was pope, that at some point he must have read the beatitudes. So is he saying the beatitudes are crap? All that stuff about the poor in spirit and the meek? "Nonsense!!" he says. "What it's all about is strict discipline." I mean, how can you take Jesus's teaching and come up with "kindness is for fools"?

Then there's a form of Christianity where they seem to believe that if you pray enough, you get lots of money. There's always been a sort of sense in America that Christianity is the cornerstone of capitalism. That's what we're about—we're really a good Christian, capitalist, competitive society. What does a spiritual teacher have to say that can't get screwed up by people like that? The answer is he can't. Somebody once said, "An idea is not responsible for the people who hold it."

See, we have this absolutely extraordinary situation where the founder of the religion lays something down and, of course, he's able to really explain it to people around him, and they're able to explain it to the next four or five generations who are really dedicated to the teachings. But later on, priests start joining the abbey because the food is good. Do you see what I mean?

It's important to remember that you have to be at a certain level of spiritual advancement before you can understand some of the ideas. I mean, when Christ said, "Turn the other cheek," he was not teaching a trick, although people with certain cast of mind would think it must be some kind of manipulation because, surely, he can't really have meant that. So you have to be at a certain level in order to understand the subtler teachings, and most people don't reach anything like that level. What I like about Buddhism is that they insist on the oral transmission, and the teachers become remarkable people. I met the Dalai Lama a few times, and there's no question that he's operating on a different level from me, in the same way I'm operating on a higher level than the average *Daily Mail* journalist.

SMITH: Do you believe in an afterlife?

CLEESE: Yes, I do. But I don't know what it is. I was a member of a group that met in California for a week every year and I went there for eight years. They were all academics, most of them psychologists or social psychologists. One was a very famous quantum physicist who did not think there was any contradiction between quantum physics and an afterlife, and there were philosophers and anthropologists. We studied all the evidence, and I came away after eight years thinking, "Yes, I think there is an afterlife." But the trouble comes when you try to say how it works. People start trying to draw up maps of what the afterlife is, but I don't think our minds may be capable of understanding it. But I genuinely do think something goes on. Not, perhaps, for everyone. Maybe one has to do a certain amount of work in order to gain an afterlife. I don't know. But what I like about it is, it helped me with my standard fear of death. I think now, when I'm lying on my deathbed, probably three-quarters panicked, there will be a quarter of me thinking: "Ooooh, I wonder what happens next."

You see, the key to scientific thinking is that data should outrank theory. The territory is primary to the map. If you look at some territory and then you look at a map of it and you compare them, and on the map there's a bridge and in real life there isn't a bridge, you don't say: "Well, obviously there must be a bridge." Do you see what I mean? If you look at the reality and see there *isn't* a bridge, you query, why does the map say there *is* a bridge? So the territory is primary to the map. Scientists don't behave like that. Scientists are very emotionally attached to their theories, and if anybody starts challenging a theory, they get rather angry because they like being right.

SMITH: So, we have time for one more question, from Jack Mindich: "What is the worst article you've ever seen in the *Daily Mail*?"

CLEESE: The one that annoyed me most was when I first started going out with my wife. I call her Fish because she swims like a fish. The first time I saw her swim, for forty-five minutes she went up and down the pool, and she got out and she wasn't even out of breath, and I thought, "She knows how to breathe underwater." She's the only human being I've ever met who can do that, so I call her Fish. Anyway, I'd started to go out with Fish and the *Daily Mail* ran one of its nasty pieces. One doesn't usually take it personally because it's their way of life, but this one got to me because they said about her that she used to dance naked in order to keep my interest in her up. You see? It's profoundly demeaning to her. It also raises the question, how would they know? So one has to deal with this constant flow of malicious misinformation from the *Daily Mail,* and I criticize them because they are so unscrupulous and dishonest. You must never trust them because they're quite plausible, as they chat to you until you think they're actually interested in you, and then they'll slip a question in and that's the only thing they'll ever quote from the interview.

Overall, I'm very shocked by British journalism. On the way over on the plane, I read the *New York Times*, and I read the *Sunday Times* and the *Sunday Telegraph*, and the gap in quality between the papers was absolutely breathtaking. The *New York Times*, I think, is a great paper. I read three articles in it, all of which were absolutely first-class. The *Sunday Times* is just kind of obvious and pompous. There was one very, very good piece in it by a guy called Matt Lucas, but otherwise, it was just like anything that Murdoch touches—grubby. And then there was the *Sunday Telegraph*, which is just hopeless. It's the most skewed, useless waste of trees you ever saw in your life. It's owned by a reclusive pair of twins called the Barclay Twins, who are simply interested in advertising revenue. About three years ago, they decided that the way to boost their profits was to get rid of all the good writers because they were more expensive. Now it's almost entirely run by ex-employees of the *Daily Mail*. So I despair for British journalism.

But what I love about America is there's resilience here, and centers of quality that are just as good or possibly better than what you have in most of the rest of the world. I'm absolutely delighted at the thought of being able to come back to Cornell on a regular basis and stir things up.

SMITH: Thank you very much.

# INDEX